THE NATIONAL INSTITUTE OF
ECONOMIC AND SOCIAL RESEARCH

Occasional Papers
XXIII

LANCASHIRE TEXTILES

A

The National Institute of Economic and Social Research is an independent, non-profit-making body, founded in 1938. It has as its aim the promotion of realistic research, particularly in the field of economics. It conducts research by its own research staff and in co-operation with the universities and other academic bodies. The results of the work done under the Institute's auspices are published in several series, and a list of its publications up to the present time will be found at the end of this volume.

LANCASHIRE TEXTILES

A Case Study of Industrial Change

BY

CAROLINE MILES

CAMBRIDGE
AT THE UNIVERSITY PRESS
1968

PUBLISHED BY

THE SYNDICS OF THE CAMBRIDGE UNIVERSITY PRESS

Bentley House, 200 Euston Road, London, N.W.1

American Branch : 32 East 57th Street, New York N.Y. 10022

Printed in Great Britain by Metcalfe Cooper & Hepburn Limited, London, E.C.2

CONTENTS

LIST OF TABLES

LIST OF FIGURES

CONVENTIONS AND SYMBOLS

Cotton Board and Textile Council

On January 1st, 1967, after the bulk of this study was completed, the Textile Council for the Man-made Fibre, Cotton and Silk Industries of Great Britain was created in place of the Cotton Board, which was rather more limited in coverage of both fibres and processes. The older title, Cotton Board, is used throughout the text, and in references to source material, except where specific mention is made of the new Textile Council.

Symbols used in the tables

n.a. means 'not available'
—   means 'nil'

AUTHOR'S PREFACE

This research began as part of a wider study of 'strategic factors in economic growth', initially under the direction of Mr. R. R. Neild, which the Institute undertook with the aid of a Ford Foundation grant. Mr. Neild took as a starting-point the question 'What influences the rate at which technical progress is exploited by industry?'. He decided to adopt a micro-economic approach, analyzing the different influences at work in a number of industries, and it was thought that the process of scrapping and replacement in the Lancashire textile industry, artificially stimulated as it was by the 1959 Cotton Industry Act, would make an interesting case study. For reasons explained in the Introduction, my research developed into a wider study of the industry, although the analysis of the impact of the 1959 Act remains a central feature.

Anyone outside an industry who attempts to analyze its problems in detail inevitably incurs a large number of debts. My first thanks must go to the people working in the cotton and related textile industries, in Lancashire and elsewhere, who gave of their time and their knowledge. As several of those I talked to preferred to remain anonymous, I am precluded from thanking any of them by name.

Among organizations I want to thank the Shirley Institute, the British Spinners' and Doublers' Association, the United Kingdom Textile Manufacturers' Association and, most particularly, the Cotton Board (now the Textile Council) for assistance at various stages of my research. I would like to convey a special word of thanks to the staff of the Textile Council's Statistical Department, as without their deep knowledge of the industry, and their readiness to apply it to the tedious work of analyzing the results of the 1959 Act in detail, it would not have been possible to compile the structural tables on which I have drawn extensively. In this context thanks are also due to Messrs. Binder, Hamlyn Ltd. for providing the basic information on payments of grants to firms that scrapped equipment.

Mr. E. G. W. Allen, Director of the Lancashire and Merseyside Industrial Development Association, helped to fill in the picture of what the contraction in textiles has meant to the economy of the North-Western region, and Mr. A. H. Parkinson, Industrial Development Officer of Bolton, kindly supplied me with detailed information relating to Bolton and the surrounding villages.

The Board of Trade gave much appreciated practical assistance in extracting data from microfilm records, and supplied detailed information on administrative questions.

Some of my findings have already been published in two articles in the District Bank Review: 'Contraction in Cotton: Some Comments on the 1959 Cotton Industry Act' (June 1965) and 'Should the Cotton Industry be Protected?' (June 1966). I would like to thank the editor for permission to use this material.

I am deeply grateful to Christopher Saunders and Robert Neild, then respectively Director and Deputy Director of the National Institute, for inviting me to join the staff in order to undertake this study and for their help in the early stages of my research. The Institute's present Director, David Worswick, made many helpful suggestions during the later stages of the work, and patiently read and commented on several drafts. Mrs. Anne Jackson, Secretary of the Institute, has sustained me throughout, as a professional critic of the work as it progressed, in dealing with various practical problems connected with my research and latterly in preparing the manuscript for the press.

Finally on a more personal note, I want to thank Derek and Elisabeth Russell for their warm hospitality on my many visits to Lancashire, Stephen Hyde for reading the manuscript with great care and saving me from many stupid mistakes (he is not, of course, responsible for those that remain) and my husband for his constant encouragement and support.

CAROLINE M. MILES

London, July 1967

INTRODUCTION

The present study of recent changes in the Lancashire textile industry has grown out of a larger project, as explained in the preface. The aim of the larger project, a study of 'strategic factors in economic growth', was to identify factors determining the rate of growth and progress in a mature economy which might be influenced by public policy or by practicable changes in attitudes; a micro-economic approach was adopted and the process by which, and the conditions under which, obsolescent and inefficient units of production give way to new ones was taken to be of central interest.

The line of thought was this. On the one hand, the idea that the transfer of labour from old to new vintages of equipment is of key importance to growth in mature economies has been emphasized in recent theoretical work.[1] On the other hand, there appeared to be evidence that in the British economy there is some surplus of capital capacity in relation to labour, and that old and inefficient plant, which could be dispensed with, continues to operate, absorbing part of the labour force which might with benefit be transferred to newer and more productive plant. In the major study, three lines of investigation were pursued. The first was a direct inquiry into replacement policy addressed to a sample of firms in the metal goods industries.[2] The second was to examine the dispersion of 'efficiency' between plants and between industries with the aid of census data and to see if this dispersion seemed excessive.[3] The third was to investigate in depth the relationship between technical progress and replacement policies in particular industries. The two selected were coal-fired electricity generation, an industry with a homogeneous product and one in which technical progress, age of plant, and productivity would be relatively easy to observe[4]; and Lancashire textiles, which offered a special opportunity to survey the conception, application and results of a recent government rationalization scheme intended to promote extensive scrapping and re-equipment.

The theoretical starting-point for these several industry studies has been the hypothesis that, given an existing stock of capital equipment of

---

[1] See, for example, *Productivity and Technical Change* by W. E. G. Salter (Cambridge, 1960).

[2] R. R. Neild, 'Replacement policy', *National Institute Economic Review*, No. 30, November 1964.

[3] A paper on this part of the study is being revised for publication by Professor F. P. R. Brechling, formerly a member of the team at the National Institute.

[4] One paper on the electricity generating industry has already been published: 'An international comparison of production techniques: the coal-fired electricity generating industry' by F. P. R. Brechling and A. J. Surrey, *National Institute Economic Review*, No. 36, May 1966.

varying ages and efficiencies, and assuming full employment, output will grow at a rate determined by the rate at which labour is shifted from less to more technically efficient and productive equipment. The least efficient plant is then 'knocked out' and retired from use. Growth of output in this way will automatically be accompanied by rising productivity of labour, given the full employment assumption, and the productivity of capital may also increase, though it will not necessarily do so.

One obvious defect of this hypothesis is that in the real world the assumption of full employment is most unlikely to hold completely for a firm or an industry, even if it does hold at the level of the economy. A firm or an industry may be able to grow without any change in its existing productive techniques, but simply by installing more of the same kind of plant and equipment, if it can recruit more workers from other firms in the industry or from other industries. Although the possibilities of obtaining additional labour are limited by several factors, including geographical immobility, the problem of technical training and union attitudes, it is clear that both firms and industries do expand in this way even in a fully employed economy.

An important assumption underlying the theoretical model is that total costs of production using 'new' equipment will be lower than costs using 'old' equipment, at the level of output that the firm or industry can expect to attain. Since much industrial research and development is concentrated on the search for cost-reducing techniques, it may seem surprising that this assumption needs emphasis. But if costs using 'new' equipment can only be minimized by doubling the firm's present level of output, for example, the firm may have no reason to re-equip unless it can see the possibility of rapidly increasing its level of sales. And where the total market for the products of the industry in which the firm is operating is stagnant or only growing slowly, this possibility may be remote unless the changes in the price and/or the quality of product produced with 'new' equipment are sufficiently great to give the firm a major competitive advantage, or the firm is able to buy out some or all of its main rivals.

This sort of technical barrier to modernization, arising from the indivisibility of units of capital equipment, is primarily a problem for the small firm, and the small firm is most unlikely to possess or be able to draw on the financial resources needed to alter the structure of the industry in which it is operating. But bigger firms may also find that they cannot achieve optimal cost levels with 'new' equipment unless they can expand sales, and if the difference in 'old' and 'new' costs is not very large, if the product is not homogeneous, and if the market is not easily controlled, firms with widely differing efficiencies, measured in terms of the productivities of various inputs, will co-exist. Considerable problems thus arise in applying the kind of model outlined here to an analysis of growth and industrial change in an industry with a large number of firms of differing sizes and efficiencies.

Further difficulties crop up where the industry's output is not homogeneous, and its composition is continually changing. If the nature of an industry's output is changing over time, which is perhaps the case more often than not, productivity comparisons over time may have little meaning. And if an industry is defined in terms of the markets it is supplying rather than its productive techniques, major changes in the productivity of labour in the industry may occur as the result of the application of entirely new techniques to the production of substitutes rather than step-by-step improvements in existing techniques.

In analyzing the processes of change in the textile industry, there are major practical as well as conceptual problems. Although the range and quality of statistical information is a good deal better than for many other industries, mainly because of the authority given to the Cotton Board under the 1947 Development Councils Act to compel all firms in the industry to make regular statistical returns, some important series are lacking altogether. Thus, although there are statistics on the main types of machinery installed, there is nothing on dates of installation. And the labour statistics, although internally consistent, do not reveal the extent of short-time working or unemployment, and are so different in coverage from the Ministry of Labour statistics for the industry that official short-time and unemployment percentages cannot be applied with any confidence to Cotton Board data.

But the main shortcoming is the lack of information on output by size of firm. For the purposes of the present study it has been possible, with the assistance of the statistical department of the Cotton Board, to obtain a picture of the size distribution of firms in the industry, using employment as a measure of size, for the period immediately before the passage of the 1959 Act and for a recent period. There are, however, no available data on output by size of firm[1]. It is thus impossible to determine the relationships, if any, between size and labour productivity, or between vintages and types of equipment and labour productivity.

As the textile study got under way it became increasingly clear that in order to understand the impact and results of the 1959 rationalization measures they had to be considered in a wide economic and historical context. For a start it was necessary to look at the concept of industrial change in a declining industry. In what sense is progress possible—or does it actually occur—when output is falling? Chapter 1 discusses this

---

[1] Even if such data were available, they would need to be interpreted with very great care, in view of the heterogeneous nature of the textile industry's output. See chapter 2.

question, and presents an analytical framework for the study. It also seemed necessary, in a study concerned with technical progress, to look at the actual processes of textile manufacture, the ways in which improvements in efficiency can be obtained, and at recent technological development. These matters are dealt with in Chapter 2. Chapter 3 describes the historical background to the situation that existed in 1959; and discusses previous official attempts, over the last 30 years, to assist the adaptation of the industry to its declining circumstances. The objectives, implementation and immediate results of the 1959 Cotton Industry Act are dealt with in Chapter 4, and some critical comments on it are offered in Chapter 5. The last chapter looks at what has been happening in the industry in the 1960's, and attempts to put recent developments, including major changes in structure and important shifts in the pattern of fibre consumption, into perspective. It concludes with a look at some of the problems the industry is facing now.

An Appendix to the study examines the effects of contraction in textiles on the economy of the region, and discusses some of the attempts made to diversify the industrial structure of the old cotton towns.

Finally, in this introduction, it seems appropriate to add a warning about some of the generalizations that are made in the study, and an apology to those who may, with reason, feel irritated by them. The performance and behaviour of the industry, and the nature of the Government's response to its difficulties, are open to criticism on many counts. Problems and external conditions have been misunderstood, and wrong decisions taken. But the author is aware that throughout the difficult period of stagnation and decline for the industry as a whole there have been individuals and enterprises making the effort to adjust to changing circumstances, and adopting clear-headed and rational attitudes towards management and technological problems. The author apologizes to these individuals and firms for not always explicitly exempting them from critical generalizations that do not in fact apply to them. And readers who assume that the industry has only itself to blame for all its difficulties should be warned that neither diagnosis nor cure is so simple.

CHAPTER I

THE FRAMEWORK OF THE STUDY

The purpose of this essay is to present and discuss the results of a case study of industrial change. Much of it, therefore, is factual and descriptive, concerned with the structure and organization of the industry at various points during the period of change, with the sequence of events and with the factors that seem to have been promoting or inhibiting change. But the study was begun with some specific questions about the nature of industrial change in mind, and the first part of the present chapter is devoted to an analysis of its framework. This analysis does not presume to develop a general model of industrial change, but rather sets out the thinking that has determined the collection and guided the interpretation of the factual material.

A great deal of attention is currently given to analysing change and growth at the level of the economy, and there has been some interesting theoretical work, though little empirical study in this country at any rate, on the ways in which firms grow. But there is practically nothing about industrial change. Works on individual industries tend to concentrate on describing changes in structure without trying to account for them in a very coherent way: various factors are identified, including international competition, the prevailing structure, and technical progress, but the inter-relatedness of these factors is not made clear. One important reason for this failure is the difficulty of arriving at a valid definition of an industry which will permit an analysis of the structural, organizational and technical changes that are taking place within the group of firms that are identified as belonging to this industry, a point to which we shall return.

For the present, leaving on one side the problem of defining an industry, we are concerned with the general concept of industrial change or industrial progress. Industries—or rather forms of industrial activity—do of course decline, but we shall be concerned not so much with the understanding of why certain activities decline as why new activities and techniques arise within the same industry. We shall start with a definition of the term industrial progress.

The term industrial progress has been chosen with care, to indicate the concept of an improvement in the method of production of the industry's output, or in other words an increase in the efficiency of the industry. It is thus not the same thing as industrial growth, or an expansion of output, which could theoretically be achieved by simply increasing the amounts of all inputs in the same proportions as they are employed at the present time, with no change in techniques or methods of organization. If there was no technical progress, industrial growth could only be obtained this way. It seems, however, that in practice most industrial growth includes an element of industrial progress in the sense in which we are defining it. Nevertheless it is conceptually useful to distinguish between industrial growth and industrial progress, in order to emphasize the element of change in the latter. A second important aspect of the distinction is that it is perfectly possible to envisage industrial progress without growth of output.

This does not imply, however, that industrial progress can be simply equated with technical progress, if this term is given its usual meaning. Technical progress is commonly taken to refer to the absorption of scientific discoveries and technological developments into the actual productive process, resulting in a reduction of the quantities of inputs (labour, material, sometimes capital) per unit of output, and also, or alternatively, an improvement in the quality of output. In view of its physical nature it will be evident that such progress can only occur in an actual production unit. And it will only occur if the embodied technical improvements lead to cost advantages that the individual firm is equipped and prepared to exploit. No firm, for example, will, or perhaps one ought to say should, invest in labour-saving equipment unless it can reduce its total unit costs, not just its unit labour costs, thereby.

Technical progress takes place in individual plants and improvements in management and organization at the level of the firm. Industrial progress, on the other hand, is the sum of the technical and other changes in all the firms that make up an industry. While industrial progress may occur without expansion of total output, it cannot occur without technical progress, and its rate is affected by the rate of technical progress. But it is also affected by other factors, of which an important one is the rate of progress of the technically progressive firms compared with the rest of the industry.

This brings us to the need to examine the concept of an industry. There are three possible ways of defining an industry; in terms of its principal raw material inputs, in terms of its production processes, or in terms of its range of outputs. The first of these is the oldest, and despite its obvious limitations, it is still widely used. We have a tobacco industry, a food processing industry, and indeed some people would still say a cotton industry and a woollen industry. The second approach to definition, through the nature of the productive processes used, is the one most frequently adopted at the present time, by official statisticians and others. At first sight it seems peculiarly suited to the discussion of technical progress and related problems, as it is based precisely on the techniques of industrial production, the ways in which a group of similar raw materials are turned into a group or groups of recognizably related manufactured products. The third approach to definition, in terms of end-products, has the great advantage that it concentrates attention on the reason for an industry's existence, namely that it produces a range of goods or services that the community wants, and does so more efficiently than individuals working for themselves could do. However it does lead to major difficulties in classification. It seems to be harder to find the gaps in the chain of substitution over the whole range of output than it is to find divisions between different kinds of productive process or different sorts of input. Despite this, there is a detectable shift towards a recognition of the fact that the analysis of industrial problems must proceed from the product end as well as from the starting point of the techniques of industrial production. We are beginning to think in terms of a power industry and a transport industry and, perhaps, a defence industry, and to emphasize the importance of end-uses as well as of inputs and processes.

In order to decide which of these approaches to the problem of defining an industry is the most useful, it is necessary to consider the purpose of evolving a definition—any definition—in the first place. The primary unit we are dealing with is the enterprise or firm or establishment that is manufacturing products or supplying a stream of services: in defining an industry we are trying to classify these primary units in some meaningful way. One test of a good definition, then, must be the proportion of difficult cases it gives rise to—the more the cases, the worse the definition, since the object of the definition is to sort out a large number of units into certain broad categories. A second test is the relevance of the definition to the subject of the analysis: if this is concerned with the effect of changes in the price of a major input, for example, the definition must clearly include all firms using this input, even if they produce highly diverse end-products.

If we apply these two tests to the second and third approaches listed— the process-orientated and the market-orientated definitions—we come up with a rather mixed answer. By the first test, a market definition fails, as it throws up a large number of marginal cases among firms producing for diverse end-uses. To take an example from the textile industry, a weaving firm might very well produce furnishing fabrics on 50 per cent of its looms and tyre fabrics on the other 50 per cent. Should it then be classified as being in the household goods industry or the motor industry? On the other hand if the same firm is classified according to the processes it uses, no problem arises.[1]

By the second test, however, a market definition begins to look much

---

[1] The problem of firms with diverse processes can sometimes, though not always, be got round by classifying individual productive establishments rather than firms, as is the Census practice.

more useful. The process definition may appear to be highly relevant to the problems of technical progress, but is this really the case? Just to group together the units that are using the same set of techniques at a given point in time, and whose progress may therefore be viewed as starting from a common point, tells us nothing, of itself, about why some firms advance from this base while others do not. And the factors that are brought in to account for these differences, including managerial ability, access to capital, and so on, lead us inevitably into consideration of the whole market structure in which the firm is operating. Here it may be up against firms using quite different raw materials and processes to produce competing end-products. The packaging industry, using paper, plastics, metals and glass, is a good example of this.

The two types of definition overlap to a very great extent. Thus most textile firms produce for one of three end-uses: clothing, household goods and specialized industrial purposes, particularly for the transport industry, and for none of these uses do they have any serious competition from other kinds of producers at the present time. However it is when one moves on to a finer product classification that the difference between the two types of definition becomes more significant: it seems more meaningful to regard the producers of woven and knitted fabrics as being in competition with each other in the apparel market than the producers of woven apparel fabrics as being in competition with other producers of woven fabrics for the industrial market.

Accordingly one is driven to adopt a hybrid definition. In what follows, an industry is defined as a group of firms using similar or sub-stitutable processes to produce a competing range of end-products. Thus the textile industry is defined as the group of firms producing textile products for all apparel, household goods and transport and other industrial uses. Such a definition is of course partly circular and tauto-logical, but it at least does not exclude the possibility that new uses for textile products will lead to the development of a new branch of the industry, or that new techniques will invade and capture existing markets for its products.

A framework for the analysis of industrial change

We are concerned with the analysis and measurement of industrial change, or the rate of industrial progress within an industry. Before beginning to try to identify the various factors that promote or inhibit industrial progress, we may look at the different ways in which this progress can be measured.

It will be recalled that industrial progress as defined is not the same thing as growth of output and further, that it is possible to have progress without growth. The rate of growth, then, is of no use as a measure of industrial progress. It will further be recalled that industrial progress is the result of the technical and other changes that take place in all the firms comprising the industry. What is needed, therefore, is some measure of the effects of all these changes, some measure of the efficiency with which the industry produces its output. Two groups of measures suggest themselves. The first, and perhaps the most obvious, is efficiency in the use of one or several inputs per unit of output. In practice the unit that is most often chosen is labour, but it could be either raw materials or capital. Whatever the unit of input used, care must be taken to ensure that as far as possible it is a constant unit, or in other words that its quality remains unchanged.

The second and perhaps less obvious group of measures relates to financial performance. Here the conceptual and practical difficulties in the way of finding adequate yardsticks are formidable. But it nevertheless seems important not to lose sight of the fact that a major objective of the progressive firm is to maintain, and if possible increase, the rate of return on the capital it employs. A firm that concentrates on increasing its labour productivity without paying close attention to its total costs and sales, and finds itself in a situation where the yield on total capital employed is declining, which may happen even if turnover is increasing, is doubtfully progressive. How far a firm can actually increase its rate of return over a number of years is of course significantly affected by the conditions governing entry into the industry. Changes in an industry's average rate of return over time are also determined to some extent by the conditions governing entry and exit, as well as by the performance of the firms in the industry. The rate may also be altered by changes in external factors, such as a shift in the levels of tariffs or sales taxes, for example.

For the present, however, while recognizing its limitations, we shall discuss the ways in which industrial progress can occur in terms of a single measure of change, namely the productivity of labour.

Changes in the productivity of labour take place at different rates within different firms, the weighted average of these rates giving the rate of change for the industry as a whole. Thus it seems that the most obvious way in which an industry can progress is through increased productivity in individual firms. But progress can occur without any change in the productivity of individual firms, if the composition of the group of firms making up the industry alters—if, for example, the 10 per cent of firms with the lowest labour productivities go out of business. In fact, in an industry with a large number of firms operating under competitive conditions, one might expect both mechanisms to be at work— the productivity of leading firms rising *and* the most inefficient firms leaving the industry—but it is useful to keep the distinction between the two mechanisms in mind.

The model of industrial change developed by Salter and others postulates, in its simplest form, that industrial progress occurs—or efficiency improves—as labour is shifted from old to new vintages of capital equipment that are assumed to embody technical improvements intended, amongst other things, to increase the productivity of labour. Stated in these broad terms, the model has the attraction of describing reality at its most favourable. Firms do increase their efficiency by investment in new equipment, and do increase output per man by putting men to work on more productive equipment. But what is of interest is to examine the conditions necessary for this sort of transfer to take place, both within firms and among firms in an industry. It may be that some firms in an industry are actually retrogressing, if they are using old plant and the frequency of repairs is increasing, and if this is the case the efficiency of the industry as a whole may be unchanged, or even, conceivably, falling, although there are progressive firms in it.

These conditions fall into four inter-related groups: the character of technical innovation; the existence of market conditions favourable to forward-looking investment policies; the price and the mobility, in all senses, of labour; and lastly the capacity of management.

The character of technical innovation cannot be assumed to be constant for all industries all the time. It may be the case that except in obsolescent industries there is a more or less continuous stream of minor modifications and improvements to existing processes that over a period can lead to considerable increases in productivity, but periods of major technical innovation are often widely separated in time, at least in older industries. In textiles, for example, there was a great flowering of invention between about 1760 and about 1830, and then few significant new inventions for over a hundred years, until the developments of the last decade, some of which, for example the Sulzer loom, have their origins in technical research carried out in the 1930's. However, even at a time when there is a rapid flow of new technical innovations offering major cost advantages to the firm prepared to invest in new plant, the actual rate of technical progress in individual firms will not be high unless all the other conditions are right. Amongst these conditions are the market situation and the labour situation, discussed in subsequent paragraphs, but there is also the problem of technical complementarity. It may be impossible, for purely technical reasons, to re-equip for one stage of a production process without re-equipping for other earlier or subsequent stages. To take an example from the textile industry, it is impracticable to introduce modern equipment for the processes preparatory to spinning unless the spinning process itself is already carried out on modern ring spindles, or ring spindles are installed at the same time. The product of the 'shortened processing techniques' is not suitable for spinning on mules. So a firm that has not undertaken any re-equipment for some time—in the terms of the present example, the firm still using mule spindles—finds that it has to re-equip right through its plant or not at all.[1] This means that the level of capital expenditure required is larger than for the firm that has already installed the necessary complementary equipment, and helps to explain, amongst other things, why firms that are already backward, in a technical sense, find it increasingly hard to catch up.

A second major factor affecting re-equipment decisions is the scale and probable rate of growth of the markets open to the firm. If the market is expanding fast, and if a firm expects to be able to reduce its costs and its selling prices substantially, through re-equipment, and thus obtain a larger share of this market, the incentive to reinvest will be strong. But at the opposite extreme, if the total market is stagnant or shrinking, and the cost savings to be obtained from re-equipment are small, the firm has not much incentive to invest. Even under optimum conditions investment in new plant is a risk—projections of demand and cost-saving calculations may turn out to have been too optimistic, or external conditions may change—and the more uncertain the future, the riskier it becomes. In addition, there may be special circumstances, such as a minimum price agreement that in effect stabilizes market shares, and protects high-cost producers.[2]

Perhaps the most important element in capital re-equipment decisions is labour: its availability, price and readiness to adapt to new tasks. It is a striking feature of most of the quantitative studies of the cost savings to be obtained from re-equipment in the textile industry that, although the main emphasis is placed on the labour cost savings obtainable, the actual reduction in total costs, when allowance is made for depreciation of new plant, is often worked out to be small or non-existent.[3] This rather surprising conclusion, also reached by Sutherland in the study cited, suggests that at the time most of these studies were made the price of labour did not fully reflect its scarcity, or alternatively that there was no real shortage of labour. Given full employment the processes of industry-wide collective bargaining may perhaps have tended to keep wages lower than they would be under 'free' market conditions, and so have made it possible for inefficient, labour-intensive producers to remain in the industry. However, if there is an absolute and persistent shortage

[1] This example is taken from Alister Sutherland, 'The Diffusion of an Innovation in Cotton Spinning', *Journal of Industrial Economics*, vol. VII, no. 2., March 1959.

[2] The effects of such an agreement are discussed in Sutherland, *op. cit.*

[3] References to the technical literature will be found in the next chapter, where the nature of technical progress in the textile industry is discussed in some detail.

of labour, industry-wide arrangements tend to be overtaken by plant bargaining, and a situation may develop where re-equipment becomes increasingly attractive both in terms of reducing unit costs and in terms of maintaining or expanding output.   A further factor in the labour situation is the readiness of labour to adapt itself to new methods of working, both formally through the abandonment of demarcation and other restrictive agreements and informally in its readiness and capacity to undergo training.   Major re-equipment may have far-reaching effects on the whole pattern of demand for labour, men displacing women for example, or men with engineering training displacing skilled craftsmen.

Finally, we come to the requirement that management must be seeking to progress.   If all industries were composed of firms producing homogeneous products for sale in perfectly competitive markets the choice for management would be to progress or die, but in the real world, where such conditions do not prevail, it becomes possible for firms with a wide range of efficiencies to survive.   In economic terms, the main explanation for this may be the imperfections of the market, but it is impossible to ignore the considerable body of evidence, from many industries, that points to the conclusion that many managers do not want to grow, and do not necessarily want to put their competitors out of business.   What makes a manager decide actively to seek increased efficiency in production from a 'static' position is difficult to discover: what does seem clear, however, is that the influences at work in different situations are themselves varied, and that non-economic forces, as well as economic considerations, play a considerable part in management's decision making processes.

CHAPTER 2

TEXTILE PROCESSES AND TECHNOLOGY

A firm can increase its productive efficiency through the application of improved technology, through the rationalization of its product structure, or through the re-organization of its management. Often, firms find themselves obliged to do all three things in order to maximize the benefits obtainable from any one of them. In order to understand the alternatives open to firms seeking increased efficiency, which are discussed subsequently in this chapter, it is necessary first to look at the actual sequence of manufacturing processes. Only by examining the steps in the process of turning raw fibre into finished cloth do the technical possibilities for reducing labour and other costs per unit of output become apparent. Particular emphasis is therefore given to the kinds of work that textile operatives have to perform.

1. THE PROCESSES OF TEXTILE MANUFACTURE

In an industry with as many variations in productive techniques as the Lancashire textile industry, no short account of the process of manufacture can be fully comprehensive. The basic description is of average to good techniques, but not 'best practice' techniques, as used in 1964–5, when the author's own first hand observations were made. The general range of techniques available at each stage of the process is also briefly indicated, but modern 'best practice' techniques, the adoption of which is very much bound up with re-organization of product and management structure, are discussed in the following section in connection with an examination of the nature of technical progress in the textile industry.

First it is necessary to identify the main types of fibre used, as by their nature they require processing in different ways. Cotton is, of course, the fibre on which the industry's technology has been founded, and it is still quantitatively the most important, accounting for 57 per cent by weight of total yarn consumed in 'Lancashire' weaving in 1966. Man-made fibres account for virtually all the rest. From the point of view of their origins these can be divided into two broad categories, the cellulosic fibres such as rayon that are vegetable derivatives, and the true synthetic fibres such as nylon and terylene that are manufactured from inorganic raw materials. But from the point of view of technology a more significant distinction is between staple and continuous filament fibres; while staple fibres, like cotton, must be spun into yarn before they can be woven or knitted into cloth, continuous filament fibres are by definition produced as yarns and do not have to be spun. Both sorts of fibres, cellulosic and synthetic, are used in both staple and continuous filament forms. The description of the spinning process that follows therefore applies to cotton and staple fibres, and the description of weaving and finishing to all three types of fibre. The variations in treatment each fibre requires in these different processes are not of sufficient importance to merit description in the present context.

The three main steps in the production of woven cloth[1] are spinning, weaving and finishing. While the first two of these are self-explanatory, the third needs a word of explanation. Virtually all cloth leaving a weaving shed needs some further processing, ranging from bleaching, dyeing or printing in the case of 'grey' cloth to cutting, folding and otherwise preparing for delivery to consumers cloths woven from finished yarns. In addition to these three main processes there are a number of preparatory and intermediate processes that are of considerable significance in assessing the efficiency of a textile plant. Some of them, such as winding and spooling, are mainly directed towards getting the yarn into an appropriate shape and size of package for the next stage in the manufacturing process proper, and result in little if any change in the properties of the yarn itself, while others do modify its characteristics. This second group includes the preparation of yarn for weaving, which usually includes strengthening by a chemical process.

Raw cotton arrives at the spinning mill packed into large bales, graded according to type and length of staple. Before it can be spun it has to be cleaned and the fibres separated by carding—passing them over a large revolving cylinder covered with teeth. The individual fibres are then prepared for spinning by passing them through drawframes which straighten them out and lay them parallel in a soft rope— the 'sliver'. The sliver is next passed through speed-frames (sets of rollers running at differing speeds) to draw it out further, and is finally attenuated and twisted at the spinning frame.

Figure 2.1 shows the number of stages involved in a standard modern spinning system (column A), compared with the traditional Lancashire system (column B). Column A represents good modern practice for medium and coarse yarns: an extra passage of the sliver through a draw frame may be used for fine yarns.

The actual process of spinning is now mainly carried out on ring spindles, which twist and wind the yarn simultaneously. Up to the middle 1950's, however, mule spindles, which twist and wind the yarn alternately, predominated in Lancashire, although they had largely fallen out of use in the cotton textile industries of the other principal

---

[1] The development of knitting as a technique of fabric production is discussed in chapter 6.

Figure 2.1 Modern and traditional cotton spinning systems in Lancashire

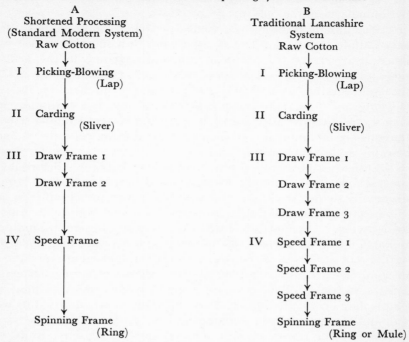

Note : Each arrow represents a movement of material that may be made manually or mechanically, usually all manually on the traditional Lancashire system.

industrialized countries. Mule spinning, besides being slower than ring spinning, also requires skilled male labour to operate the mules, and produces a yarn less suitable for subsequent automatic processing—because less strong—than ring spun yarn. In 1965, 15 per cent of the running spindles in the U.K. cotton industry were mules, but the proportion of yarn produced by them was certainly much lower than this, partly because of their slower rate of production and partly because only 12 per cent of them were running more than one shift, compared with about 53 per cent of ring spindles.

The cotton waste discarded during spinning is sufficiently great in volume, and sufficiently valuable—it may be worth 10 per cent or more of the original value of the raw cotton used—to be worth collecting and selling to specialized waste spinners, who turn it into a soft, coarse yarn for which various uses are found. The processes involved in waste spinning are not so different from those used in ordinary spinning as to require a separate description. Nor is the process of spinning man-made fibres. Here the main difference is that the fibre arrives at the spinning mill clean and cut into staple of the required length, thus eliminating the preliminary cleaning and sorting processes.

Yarn spinning is itself a completely mechanical process, at least where ring spindles are used. The manual work in a spinning mill is of three kinds: transferring the material from one machine to the next, tying together the broken ends of the thread, and maintaining the machinery in good working order. Jobs grouped under this heading range from cleaning and oiling the equipment to ensuring that optimum external conditions of temperature and humidity and correct running speeds and tensions are maintained, and include general technical supervision of the working area.

Yarn leaves the spinning frame wound on bobbins. Before it can be processed further, it almost always has to be rewound into larger and differently shaped packages, a process that may also help to even out any imperfections and make its tension more uniform—of great importance for weaving. The number of times the yarn has to be rewound depends mainly on its final purpose (for weaving, knitting, lace manufacture, etc.) as different processes (weaving or knitting) and different types and makes of equipment require different sizes and shapes of yarn packages. The integrated firm producing yarn for use in its own weaving and knitting plants may be able to reduce its winding costs, particularly if its weaving and knitting machinery is standardized.

Besides being rewound, yarn destined for weaving may also be treated in other ways. In particular, the yarn used for the warp threads of a woven cloth (the lengthways threads) must be sized in order to make it strong enough to stand the force of the weaving process, and it must also be wound onto 'beams'—large metal cylinders from which the warp unrolls onto the loom. The way in which the sizing and beaming processes are carried out is determined by the width of the looms and beams, the length of cloth of a given type to be produced—and hence the size and weight of the filled beam—and, once again, the organization and technical equipment of the firm. Not all weaving firms carry out all their own beaming.

About a fifth of the yarn (including waste yarn) consumed in cotton weaving in 1965 was doubled, by twisting two or more strands of single yarn together. Doubling, although distinguished as a separate section of the industry, may be regarded as a specialized form of winding, and does not incorporate any important new technical features or problems. Some cotton yarn, and a good deal of man-made fibre yarn, is also bleached and, or alternatively, dyed before weaving. This does not affect the weaving process but does reduce the number of subsequent cloth finishing operations.

The main preparatory processes for weaving are thus the preparation of the warp and the organization of the weft supply in a suitable form. The techniques of warp preparation do not vary significantly for different types of looms, though high speed looms require a particularly strong and uniform tension warp for efficient operation, and there may also be a problem of ensuring an adequate supply of new warps to the loom. The method of weft preparation does, however, depend on the type of loom. On the Lancashire loom, the supply of weft to the shuttle has to be replenished by hand. On an automatic loom, the weft is supplied automatically, and in some types the 'pirns'—small bobbins of weft that drop into the shuttle—are themselves wound automatically on the loom. Some of the Lancashire looms still running have been fitted with automatic attachments for weft replenishment.[1] The most advanced types of loom, such as the Sulzer and the Draper, dispose with a heavy weft-carrying shuttle altogether, the weft being carried across the warp a thread at a time, by various mechanisms. Other new types of loom under development include looms using air and water to carry the weft across the warp. At the opposite extreme, as far as speed is concerned, are the looms used to produce fancy types of cloth, such as jacquard looms, which can be 'programmed' to weave repeating patterns. The product of these looms is so different that their performance is not comparable with that of a loom producing standard cloth of the type used for sheeting or poplins, for example.

As in spinning, the main work of the operatives breaks down into handling—if the supply of weft to non-automatic looms is included in this category of occupations—tying broken threads in the weft or warp, and general mechanical maintenance of the machinery and working area. In firms producing special cloths such as brocades and multi-coloured patterns there is however still a substantial element of craft and skill required, and it seems unlikely that this will be entirely replaced by mechanical methods if the demand for these special fabrics continues, as one may expect it will, in various forms and fashions.

Three 'wet' processes—bleaching, dyeing and printing—make up the bulk of cotton and man-made fibre fabric finishing operations. About 15 per cent of the woven cloth produced is treated by various 'dry' processes that change the nature of the surface, and in addition an increasing amount of cloth is given special properties such as water-repellency, crease-resistance, flame-resistance, and so on, by specially developed finishing processes. Most of the processes, wet and dry, are largely discontinuous, and with printing, in particular, craft skills are

[1] In September 1961, the date of the most recent loom census, out of the 159,000 cotton and man-made fibre looms installed in Great Britain, 48,000 (30 per cent) were fully automatic and 3,000 Lancashire looms (2 per cent) had been fitted with automatic attachments.

required. The main exception is bleaching, which can be carried out using continuous-process equipment, though few British firms have installed this. Dyeing can also be carried out by continuous-processing methods if the pattern of orders permits it.

2. RECENT TECHNOLOGICAL DEVELOPMENTS AND THEIR APPLICATION BY THE INDUSTRY

Within the last fifteen years there have been a number of major innovations in methods of textile production and processing. Detailed accounts have appeared in the technical literature, and it is not proposed to try to describe them all here.[1] However, it may be useful to attempt a broad analysis of the main lines of development, and the chief benefits resulting from each. First, and rather apart from the stream of innovations in the textile industry proper, comes the development of new fibres, both cellulosic and synthetic. The two main cellulosic fibres, viscose rayon and acetate, have both been in use in the textile industry for most of this century, but recent developments have produced modifications of them with new properties, including the brand-named fibres Evland, Durafil, Vincel and Tricel. The best-known and quantitatively most important synthetic fibre is nylon, but among the others now used on a large scale are the polyesters (Terylene and Dacron), the acrylics (Courtelle, Orlon and Acrilan), and the polypropylenes (Ulstron), which have elastic properties. Rayon was originally produced as a cheap substitute for silk. But the chief attraction of all the other fibres has been their special properties, such as strength in relation to weight, flame resistance, crease resistance, rather than their cost. The techniques of blending man-made and natural fibres to obtain a combination of the desirable properties of both have also received a great deal of attention.

A second different kind of scientific advance has been in the development of new methods of chemical treatment of the fibres during processing, in sizing and bleaching for example, and in analysis and control of the separate processes. These developments have been more immediately directed at improving the quality of the product than at cutting costs, but they are also connected with and have made practicable many mechanical innovations. Strong and even-tensioned yarn must be used with high speed weaving machinery, for example, if breakage rates—and thus stopped time and production losses—are to be kept low, and unless they are kept low capital costs per unit of output may rise to the point at which modern equipment is no longer economic. Similarly,

---

[1] Among the technical journals are the *Textile Weekly*, the *Textile Recorder* and the *Textile Institute and Industry*. The Shirley Institute's *Bulletin* (circulated to members only) also publishes articles on textile technology.

a low breakage-rate is important, in cost terms, in mills using modern high-draft spinning equipment.

Mechanical innovations can be divided into three groups : the development of high-speed machinery, increases in the extent of automatic control and the elimination of intermediate processes. Increased speeds may be obtainable from existing machinery, but are more likely to be achieved through major modifications or the installation of new equipment. An example of increasing automation is the replacement of Lancashire looms, on which each new length of weft wound on a 'pirn' must be inserted into the shuttle by hand, with various types of automatic loom, on which the weft is replenished, and often wound onto pirns, automatically. The sort of reduction in the number of handling operations that can be obtained by eliminating intermediate processes in spinning has been indicated in figure 2.1 (p. 15). In general, increasing the number of stages of processing carried on in a single plant and the extent to which they are integrated helps to reduce the number of intermediate processes.

Finally, there have been a number of very important innovations in fabric production techniques, of which easily the most significant and far reaching in its effects is the development of knitting to produce fabrics for all sorts of purposes besides the traditional knitted garments—hose, underwear and jerseys. Two major growth areas are warp knitted fabrics, familiar to many people made up into shirts, and double jersey fabrics, also familiar made up into dresses and suits. Another new technique that is increasingly used is fabric bonding: the joining together of two layers of fabric, or one of fabric and one of some other material, often foam rubber, to produce cloths with special properties.

While it is convenient to distinguish these various lines of technical innovation as different 'starting points', it is important to emphasize that substantial advances along any one of them have not been made in isolation. Automatic machinery working at high speeds, for example, needs not only high-quality, uniform material inputs if it is to operate economically, but also a stepped-up rate of supply, which may compel the introduction of high-speed techniques, and the elimination of manual operations at an earlier stage of processing. A high degree of technical complementarity of processes appears to exist at all stages of textile manufacture, and this is an important factor in the evaluation of re-equipment costs for any one stage, and in the argument for 'verticalisation', to which we shall return in the next section.

A characteristic feature of the British cotton industry over the last fifty years, perhaps even longer, has been its lack of interest in technological development and the use of new production methods and equipment. Some firms must of course be exempted from such criticism, as was emphasized in the introduction to this study, but they do not appear to have been sufficiently powerful, taken as a group, to exert any significant influence on the domestic textile machinery industry, which has also, with the partial exception of the sector producing spinning equipment, lagged behind world developments. Virtually all the important innovations in weaving machinery, and many advances in spinning, winding and finishing equipment have been made in other countries, including the United States, Japan, France, Germany and Switzerland.[1] And few types of modern machinery, apart from spinning equipment, are even manufactured under licence in this country.

Such evidence as is obtainable about the types and age-distribution of machinery employed in the Lancashire textile industry is discussed in subsequent chapters.[2] Unfortunately the data relate only to spinning spindles, doubling spindles and looms and no systematic information is available about other machinery used in spinning, and in preparation and finishing. However, it is clear that the rate of re-equipment has been low for most of this century, and has only been stepped up appreciably in the past few years. The main cause of the shift from mule to ring spinning and from Lancashire to automatic looms—both, in broad terms, indicators of technical advance—has been the rapid absolute decline in the number of mule spindles and Lancashire looms, rather than the installation of large numbers of new machines.

The chief economic factors underlying the low rate of investment are discussed in subsequent chapters. Among purely technical factors, the failure to re-equip on any significant scale cannot be attributed to lack of information about possibilities. The principal textile trade journals publish articles on technological developments and the economics of their application, and the industry's own central research organization, the Cotton, Silk and Man-made Fibre Research Association (the Shirley Institute), makes a great deal of technical information on processes available to its members. The Cotton Board Productivity Centre has also been concerned with informing and educating firms in the application of new technology. All the firms visited by the author, including the smallest and most technically backward, knew something about technological developments in the industry.

An examination of some of the cost studies made by the Shirley Institute and others during the past few years suggests that on the basis of any simple comparisons of production costs with 'old' and 'new'

---

[1] The managing director of one leading firm in the industry, listing the equipment required for modern integrated textile operations, includes American, French, German and Swiss machinery. All the weaving and much of the preparation equipment listed is foreign. Allan Ormerod, 'The Prospects of the British Cotton Industry', *Yorkshire Bulletin of Economic and Social Research*, vol. 15 no. 1, May 1963, table VIII).

[2] See chapter 3, p. 28, and chapter 4, p. 65.

technologies, the gains to be expected from re-equipment were small.[1] This may be partly because unrealistic assumptions about costs were built into the calculations, the impact of taxation and investment allowances being ignored as a rule, for instance, while the possibility of a general upward movement in wages was not taken into account.

In as much as such calculations influenced firms at all, and without following through a large number of cases it is impossible to know to what extent they did so, they must have been a discouraging influence. But, given the prevailing lack of growth prospects for the industry and the general economic climate in which it was functioning, this does not mean that firms acted wrongly or irrationally in deciding not to re-equip. The main conclusion of many technical studies, as of the broader enquiries into the state of the industry undertaken during the post-war period,[2] was that fundamental changes in the structure and organization of individual firms, and of the industry as a whole, were required before optimal use could be made of new technology. In concluding an analysis of the relative advantages of weaving with Sulzer (shuttleless) looms and automatic looms equipped with modern arrangements for weft supply, two technologists in the Italian industry wrote:—

'However, considering the slight differences in production costs existing between traditional automatic looms and shuttleless weaving looms and bearing in mind that the example quoted emanates from factories, in which, apart from introducing new production machinery, new policies concerning the rationalization of human labour have been adopted (that is, rationalization which has been achieved, as we have seen, by a high degree of standardization) and that the majority of the European Textile Factories are unfortunately still way below these levels, we feel that the factor which will affect the decisions of Italian Weaving Firms, at least during the course of the next 20 years, will not be so much the alternative of traditional automatic looms (with Box-Loader or Unifil) and shuttleless weaving machines, as the degree of skill with which the various concerns will succeed in mastering, in a manner more efficient than hitherto, the organization question by means of standardization of articles manufactured, which implies modifications in the sales structures and a more efficient use of modern quality control systems for the various stages of production; by means of introducing more rational production programming systems and work organization (including the use of more rapid systems for training personnel); by means of more analytical time and method studies, including work study and research concerning more adequate systems

---

[1] Studies made by the Shirley Institute are confidential to its members, and so no references to specific studies are given here.
[2] See the next chapter.

of labour remuneration and profit-sharing (piece rates, bonuses for production and efficiency, etc.) and, finally, by means of the skilful handling, on the part of the various mills, of the problem of recruitment of labour, which is becoming more and more scarce. In addition, recalling once again the case of the American Textile Industry, it appears that even for the most efficiently organized European textile concerns, remarkable potentialities still exist concerning all aspects of the problems of improvements in the organization of production elements.'[1]

By way of conclusion to this chapter we may look at an illustration of the importance of structural re-organization provided by an analysis of the problems Viyella encountered when it bought Combined English Mills in 1964.[2] C.E.M. was one of the largest spinning combines in the industry, accounting for about 5 per cent of total yarn output in 1961–63. It enjoyed a reputation for technical progressiveness, and had re-equipped on a large scale under the 1959 Act, so that by the end of 1963 all yarn production came from post-war ring frames with modern drafting systems. Yet between 1960 and 1964, although output per spindle was increased by 38 per cent and labour productivity by 25 per cent, the firm's financial position grew rapidly worse. At the time of the take-over, in September 1964, it was expecting to show a small trading profit for 1964 and a rather larger one for 1965, following on losses in the previous two years.

Table 2.1. *Combined English Mills, before and after take over and subsequent reorganization*

	Position before take over	Position mid 1966	Percentage change
Number of mills	14	7	−50
Number of spindles installed	404,000	221,000	−45
Yarn output per year (million lbs)	28	25	−11
Yarn output per spindle/year (lbs)	69.91	113.0	+61
Average running hours per week per installed spindle	58.89	110.5	+88
Number employed	3,983	2,318	−42
Yarn output per employee (lbs)	7,020	10,500	+50
Capital employed (£ millions)	8.0	3.5	−56
Stocks of yarn (£)	754,000	196,000	−74
Number of customers	735	120	−84

Source: Cummins, E., see footnote below.

[1] R. Gattermayer and E. Honegger, 'Shuttleless Looms and New Developments in Weft Supply to Traditional Looms' in *Technical Progress and Textile Marketing* (Report of the 1962 Congress of the International Federation of Cotton and Allied Textile Industries) (Zurich, 1963)
[2] E. Cummins, 'Combined English Mills, A Case Study in Rationalization' in *Viyella International*, Autumn 1966.

However, these expectations were not fulfilled. In analysing the causes of C.E.M's. poor performance, a number of adverse factors emerged. The company's assets were under-used; production was split up among too many units; its stocks were very high; it was trying to satisfy over 700 customers; and its future sales forecasts were insecurely based on past peak output rather than on any rational view of market prospects.

By the middle of 1966, as table 2.1 shows, the number of mills had been halved, stocks had been reduced by 74 per cent and the number of customers by 84 per cent, while output per employee had been increased by 50 per cent and output per spindle by over 60 per cent. And losses in 1964 and 1965 were converted into a profit in 1966.

CHAPTER 3

DEVELOPMENTS IN THE INDUSTRY, 1945–59

I. THE HISTORICAL BACKGROUND

In order to understand how the cotton industry came to be in the state it was by 1959, when the Cotton Industry Act was passed, it is essential to look back at some of its earlier history. It soon becomes clear that the problems of surplus capacity, a low rate of investment and stagnant if not declining labour productivity were nothing new in the 1950's.

We may start with the reminder that the output of the cotton industry had been declining since about 1910, as the following table illustrates:

	1882–4	1910–13	1926–8	1936–8
U.K. mill consumption of cotton (million lbs)	1,480	2,100	1,470	1,320
U.K. exports				
(i) as % world trade	82	58	39	28
(ii) as % domestic production	85	81	74	46

Source: R. Robson, *The Cotton Industry in Britain* (Macmillan, 1957).

The contraction in the inter-war years was due entirely to shrinking export markets, partly because the British industry was becoming less and less competitive and partly because an increasing number of countries outside the old industrial areas of Europe and the United States were beginning to establish their own textile industries, often behind protective barriers. These new industries were set up primarily to satisfy domestic demand in the countries concerned, but in a few instances an export trade also began to develop.

This decline left the industry with a large amount of surplus equipment. In 1930 only 58 per cent of spindles installed and 54 per cent of looms installed were in use. Between 1930 and 1937 there was a decline of 31 per cent in the number of spindles installed, and 28 per cent in the number of looms, although yarn and cloth production rose by 32 per cent and 23 per cent respectively. As a result the percentage of equipment employed rose to over 80 for both spinning and weaving, but even this improvement left a large surplus.

The problem of the disposal of the surplus was approached, for the spinning sector, by the establishment in 1936 of the Spindles Board, which was authorized to buy spindles and scrap them, the purchases being financed by a levy on the industry. In the three years of its existence, 1936–9, the Spindles Board bought up over 6 million spindles (13 per cent of the total number installed in 1935), but it could not keep up with the rate at which the industry was contracting: the percentage of spindles in use in the winter of 1938–9 fell below 70 per cent, and was lower than it had been in the winter of 1935–6, before the Board was established. No such organized assistance was forthcoming for the weaving sector—it would probably have been impossible to get agreement on levies and scrapping policies among the large number of small firms involved—and by 1938 the percentage of looms in use had fallen to 66.

During the 1939–45 war the industry was deliberately concentrated, by government action, in order to release labour and factory space for other kinds of production in the relatively safe North-Western area, and to save shipping space by reducing imports of raw cotton. Between the end of 1940 and the end of 1941 the number of spindles running fell by 46 per cent and the number of looms running by 37 per cent, while employment in the spinning and weaving sectors fell by 38 per cent and 39 per cent respectively from 1939–40 levels. By the end of the war the combined labour force of the spinning and weaving sectors was 189,000, a fall of nearly 50 per cent from the 1937 level, and yarn and cloth production had fallen to 51 per cent of their 1937 levels. But while the percentages of spindles and looms running had fallen from 83 per cent in 1937 to 67 per cent and 66 per cent respectively, the total amount of machinery in existence had fallen relatively little. There were 13 million spindles and 150,000–200,000 looms in closed mills.

2. THE SITUATION IN 1945

The period between 1945 and mid-1951 was crucial in the light of subsequent developments. During these years, despite the evident need for major rationalization and re-equipment identified by various official fact-finding groups and working parties, discussed below, the behaviour of the industry was dominated by short-term considerations arising out of the post-war boom. Demand was buoyant and the labour force greatly reduced, and in these circumstances both the industry and the government all too readily assumed that a labour shortage was the chief factor inhibiting expansion. However it seems that a shortage of modern machinery and the financial policies followed by many firms were also of significance.

(a) Demand

In 1943 the Cotton Board[1] published some estimates of the probable level of post-war trade in cotton goods. It assumed that domestic con-

[1] Which had been established, on rather different terms from those under which it operates at present, by the Cotton Industry Act of 1940. In 1948 it was re-established as a Development Council under the 1947 Industrial Development Act.

sumption would increase by 5 per cent over the average annual level of 1935–7, and derived figures for total consumption of U.K. produced cotton textiles on the basis of three different assumptions about exports, (i) that the pre-war trend (declining throughout the 1930's) would continue, (ii) that the trading conditions would get worse, (iii) that trading conditions, or at least the U.K.'s competitive position, would improve. The Board's estimates, compared with the actual out-turn in selected post-war years, are shown in table 3.1. Although the estimate of apparent domestic consumption has proved remarkably accurate, and was indeed exceeded in 1951, in the 1950's and 1960's a rising proportion of it has been met by imports, a possibility that had not been envisaged by the Cotton Board in its 1943 report. Exports averaged rather over 1,000 million square yards annually in 1949–51, better than the Cotton Board's most pessimistic estimate though not as good as its middle estimate, but have since declined, averaging 852 million square yards annually in 1952–4, and 300 million square yards in 1964–5.

Table 3.1. *Output, exports and imports of woven piece goods of cotton, man-made fibres and mixtures, in selected years, compared with Cotton Board's 1943 forecast of post-war figures*

	Home market	Exports	Total	Imports	million square yards Apparent domestic consumption
Cotton Board estimates					
(i)	2,300	1,504	3,804	a	2,300
(ii)	2,300	751	3,051	a	2,300
(iii)	2,300	2,430	4,730	a	2,300
Actual output					
1937	2,210[b]	2,106	4,316	71[c]	2,281
1946	1,725	665	2,390	18[c]	1,743
1951	2,472	1,078	3,550	473	2,945
1958	1,882	468	2,350	434	2,316
1965	1,600	300	1,900	676	2,276

Sources : Cotton Board Estimates and 1937 output figures : *Board of Trade Working Party Report : Cotton* (H.M.S.O. 1946), p. 117. Post-war output figures, Cotton Board.

a No estimates of imports were made.
b Annual average, 1935–7.
c Figures taken from Robson, *op. cit.* p. 346.

However, this is all part of the subsequent story. In the immediate post-war years the industry anticipated buoyant demand for its products in both domestic and export markets. Indeed the textile industry was singled out for special treatment in view of its export potential, and early in 1948 a special committee was set up under the auspices of the Ministry of Labour to try to increase its labour supply. The 'call-up' was suspended for cotton workers, day nurseries and nursery schools were established to attract married women back, and over 4,000 foreign workers were recruited.[1]

(b) The labour force

In 1945 there was a shortage of labour in relation to capacity, if it is assumed that all the spindles and looms shut down under the wartime concentration schemes could have been brought back into production, as is shown by the following figures:

	Spinning (including doubling)	Weaving
Percentage decline in labour force, 1937–45	45	50
Percentage decline in capacity, 1937–45	10[a]	5

Source: Cotton Board for labour force; Robson, op. cit. p. 339, for capacity.

[a] Mule equivalent, excluding waste and doubling spindles.

There was also a pronounced shift in the composition of the labour force, the total number of men employed falling by over 50 per cent, while the number of women fell by only 35 per cent. This change, coupled with the fact that the percentage of workers under 18 had fallen from 14.5 in 1937 to 10.1 in 1945, raised questions about the availability of a labour force in the future.

The Board of Trade Working Party stated the case:

'There are at present in the spinning section of the industry about 38½ million (mule equivalent) spindles and rather less than 1 million spindles for spinning waste cotton. These represent in total approximately the number of spindles operating in 1937. It is estimated that the average number of persons actually working in spinning and doubling in 1937 was 176,000 and that the average number actually working in the weaving section was 187,000. We may assume that, if operating methods as well as types and volume of product remained as in 1937, a similar number of workers would be required to operate all the present spinning mills and the balancing amount of doubling and weaving capacity. Allowing a margin of approximately 7½ per cent to cover normal absenteeism, the total labour force required on this basis would be 390,000—190,000 for spinning and doubling and 200,000 for weaving. The labour force available (i.e. "on the books" of firms) at the end of January 1946 was approximately 226,000 (spinning 92,250, doubling 25,000, weaving 108,750). That is to

[1] See Ministry of Labour and National Service Annual Reports, especially that for 1948 (Cmd 7822), pp. 36–37.

say, there was a deficit of 164,000, or 42 per cent (72,750 or 38.3 per cent in spinning and doubling and 91,250 or 45.6 per cent in weaving).'[1]

In 1943 the Cotton Board Post-war Committee had estimated that the total labour force that might reasonably be expected to be available in the immediate post-war period was 270,000. The Working Party further reduced this estimate to 250,000, and pointed out that this represented only 65 per cent of the total labour force required to staff existing spinning mills, and a related amount of weaving capacity, on a pre-war production basis. It drew the obvious deductions: that the number of mills must be reduced, plant modernized and a better utilization of available labour achieved. Of these policies, re-equipment was perhaps the most important—'No scope for economy in the use of labour to the extent necessary for bridging this gap appears to exist without a complete revolution in mechanical equipment.'[2]

Some increases in labour productivity in spinning had been obtained during the war, without any change in equipment, through redeployment. The Platt Mission, which was mainly concerned with making comparisons between British and American mill practice, found that typical mills in the coarse, medium and fine sections of the industry had increased their labour productivities by 18 per cent, 18 per cent and 22 per cent respectively.[3] There was little change between normal and wartime labour productivities in yarn preparation and weaving. Between 1945 and 1950 there was little or no further increase in labour productivity, and the level of output that could be achieved was thus directly related to the labour force that could be obtained.

(c) *The machinery position*

Although large numbers of spindles and looms were stopped during the wartime concentration, practically none of them were destroyed. In 1946 there were 38.5 million (mule equivalent) spindles in existence, of which 3.74 million were in mills still closed, and about 480,000 looms, of which nearly 200,000 were in closed sheds. The comparable figures for 1939 were 39.5 million spindles and 495,000 looms.[4]

By 1939 most of this machinery had already passed the end of its useful working life. In 1930, according to a study made by Political and Economic Planning, roughly 60–75 per cent of the installed capacity had been constructed before 1910 (the exact percentage being different for each type of machine). Between 1930 and 1944 only 5 new spinning

---

[1] *Board of Trade Working Party Report : Cotton* (1946) *op. cit.* p. 53.
[2] *ibid.* p. 64.
[3] *Report of the Cotton Textile Mission to the United States of America, March–April 1944* (The Platt Mission) (H.M.S.O., 1944) p. 3.
[4] Board of Trade, *op. cit.* pp. 38–40.

mills were erected.[1] The net decline in the number of spindles between 1930 and 1945 was 19 million mule spindles and 2.8 million ring spindles, and many more were reconditioned. But it seems doubtful that the reconditioning process resulted in much technical improvement since there seems to have been little increase in labour productivity in spinning since 1900.[2]

In the weaving sector the position was much the same. Between 1930 and 1945 the number of looms fell by 220,000 net.[3] Although according to a survey of weaving machinery in existence in September 1948 108,000 new looms were installed between 1920 and 1948,[4] it seems probable that most of them were set up in the early 1920's or between 1945 and 1948.

(*d*) *Availability of resources for re-equipment*

It seems unlikely that a lack of financial resources seriously inhibited re-equipment during this early post-war period. In the three years 1949-51 the trading profits of public quoted cotton companies, expressed as a percentage of their net assets, were 26, 32 and 39, the percentage for 1951 being nearly twice the average for all quoted companies. Historically, profit levels were high in comparison with anything experienced during the century, the only comparable period being the much shorter-lived boom after the first world war. But although the cotton companies also retained a greater proportion of their net income than did the average industrial company during the period 1949-53, 71.5 per cent compared with 60.5 per cent, their net expenditure on fixed assets was relatively less. Much of their income was used to increase their liquid assets, at a rate far higher (166 per cent) than the average quoted company.[5]

A more serious problem was the supply of equipment. The cotton Working Party had concluded that textile machinery of all types was likely to be in very short supply for some time. During the 1930's, when there had been virtually no demand from the British industry, the textile machinery makers had built up their export trade, and by 1946 were already exporting machinery again. About 90 per cent of the output of ring spinning machinery was earmarked for export orders, and about

[1] *Platt Mission Report*, p. 23.

[2] *ibid.* p. vii.

[3] Robson, *op. cit.* p. 339.

[4] *Survey of the Machinery in the Weaving Section of the Cotton Industry*, a survey undertaken by the Cotton Board at the request of the President of the Board of Trade (Manchester, 1949).

[5] See the chapter on the cotton industry, by S. R. Dennison, in *Studies in Company Finance*, edited by Brian Tew and R. F. Henderson (Cambridge, 1959). Almost all the public companies, quoted on the Stock Exchange, were spinners or spinner-weavers. The weaving sector was largely in the hands of small private firms.

a third of the 'totally inadequate' automatic loom capacity.[1] From the national point of view there was a conflict between the need to expand exports of machinery and the need to re-equip the domestic textile industry, which was regarded by the Government as an important potential foreign currency earner. This conflict does not seem to have been resolved. Some machinery was imported under special licensing arrangements and as a part of the Marshall Aid programme, but not enough to make a serious impact on the problem.

3. REPORTS OF THE PLATT MISSION AND THE BOARD OF TRADE WORKING PARTY

Two major official committees of enquiry investigated the cotton industry in 1944–45. They were the Platt Mission of 1944, which had the narrow task of advising on ways of increasing the productivity of labour in the British cotton industry on the basis of comparisons with production methods adopted in the American industry, and the Board of Trade Working Party of 1945, which had the broad task of looking at the industry's future in every respect, or rather in every respect except one, the relationship between employers and employees. However, this was not an aspect of the problem that could be wished away.

As nearly all the recommendations of these two bodies were ignored, there is not much point in discussing them at length. But certain of their findings, particularly relating to the question of labour productivity, the utilization of capacity and the scale of re-equipment needed, are significant in relation to subsequent developments.

The Platt Mission was concerned solely with the measurement of output per man-hour and the methods used to obtain high rates of output, and did not make any cost comparisons. It attempted to compare representative, rather than best practice or worst practice, mills, but in fact the standard of comparison used, American high draft ring spinning, permitted like-with-like comparisons with only a few of the very best British mills. Less than half the total spinning capacity of the British spinning industry was in ring spindles at all, compared with 99 per cent of the American industry, and of the British ring spindles, only a very small proportion were operated on the high draft system. Similarly, in weaving, the standard used was the automatic loom, then accounting for 95 per cent of American capacity, which however had to be compared with the Lancashire looms, that accounted for 95 per cent of British capacity.

The results suggested that even in comparison with the best British spinning mills, i.e. those employing the high draft ring system, the

---

[1] Board of Trade, *op. cit.* pp. 78–79.

Americans were much more efficient in their use of labour. The U.S. index of efficiency (Britain=100), varied between 140 and 170, the exact figure depending on the type of yarn being spun, while for weaving the American figures ranged between 200 and 330 (Britain=100). In yarn processing (the preparation of the spun yarn for weaving) the Americans were from 4 to 8 times more efficient than the British. By way of softening the comparison slightly, the Mission stated that yarn produced by British methods was more regular and of slightly higher quality, though it was not so strong and was unsuitable for use on automatic looms, where a low breakage rate is important.

In formulating its recommendations, the Platt Mission concentrated on the need for a complete reorganization of the structure of the British textile industry. For instance, commenting on the huge gap in efficiency in warp preparation, the Mission found that it was 'doubtful whether under the British conditions the American type of preparation equipment would be very satisfactory, but the fault clearly lies in the British industrial and commercial organization and not in the high-speed automatic machinery.'[1] In a similar vein, it found that in Britain weaving was still regarded as a craft rather than as an industry, methods having changed little for 40 or 50 years, and the manufacturers being dependent on 'a large and cheap, but nevertheless highly skilled, labour force.'[2]

Turning to a more general analysis of the cotton industry in the two countries, the Mission emphasized the following main points:

(i)   Industrial organization. The U.S. industry was vertically integrated, often right forward to the selling stage, in contrast to the horizontal structure of the British industry. The key to the organization of these vertically integrated firms was the automatic loom, to which all other processes are standardized and geared.

(ii) Standardization. Standardization of product was almost non-existent in British mills. In America, on the other hand, the Mission visited one mill that had been producing the same count of warp yarn for 15 years, thus permitting continuous operation of plant, the use of highly specialized machinery, and the establishment of accurate work-load assessments.

(iii) Shift working. A single shift of 48 hours was worked in British mills. In a typical American mill, the machinery was working 139 hours per week, in three shifts of 48 hours (allowing for some overlap).

(iv) Equipment. American plant was all modern, and constantly being replaced. About three-quarters of the plant in use in British mills was installed before 1910, i.e. was over 30 years old at the time of writing.

[1] *Platt Mission Report*, p. 27.
[2] *ibid.* p. 28.

The Mission's recommendations as to ways of increasing the productivity of labour in British cotton mills followed the lines of this analysis. Six general points were made in the Report:

(i) The need for a high degree of standardization to permit the introduction of bulk production techniques, necessitating changes in distribution as well as production methods;

(ii) Large-scale re-equipment ;

(iii) Improved working conditions, to attract a labour force ;

(iv) Closer co-operation between spinners and manufacturers (i.e. weavers);

(v) Improved scientific training of management ;

(vi) Greater economy in the use of labour.

It took the view that the changes required in the case of weaving, by introducing automatic looms, amounted to a revolution that could not easily be carried out under wartime conditions. Not only would large amounts of capital be needed, but also the resources to make the looms and the resources to build new weaving plants to house them. The Mission therefore felt that immediate efforts would have to be concentrated on improvements in yarn spinning and warp preparation techniques, and a number of technical recommendations to this effect were made in the Report. The most significant omission was any reference to the need for increased shift working, although the better utilization of labour achieved in American mills by working high-speed machinery on a three-shift basis was stressed in the general analysis. It is true that the Mission's mandate was to compare labour productivities and production methods in British and American mills and to make recommendations for the increase of British labour productivity, but it is nevertheless remarkable that having drawn the correct conclusion that major improvements in the British industry could only be brought about by complete re-equipment the Mission had not one word to say about the probable costs of re-equipment and the need for shift working if costs per unit of output were to be kept down. The whole Report strongly reflects the basic interest in craft and technique underlying the British approach, and the equally pronounced lack of interest in the economic and financial analysis of production problems.

In 1945 the President of the Board of Trade appointed a *Working Party* to examine the future prospects of the industry. Its mandate was

'to examine and enquire into the various schemes and suggestions put forward for improvements of organization, production and distribution methods and processes in the cotton industry, and to report as to the steps which should be adopted in the national interest to strengthen the industry and render it more stable and more capable of meeting competition in the home and foreign markets.'[1]

In its introductory analysis of the inter-war experience of the industry, the Working Party concentrated on four main problems. First, the labour position: the generally high level of unemployment that prevailed, coupled with a declining domestic and export demand for cotton goods, meant that short-time working, unemployment and wage reductions were common. The industry '... was relying on having at its disposal a cheap, highly skilled labour force which it could turn on, off or put on to short time at any moment.'[2] Such a record as an employer did not make it easy to recruit labour at a time of full or near-full employment, and the Working Party drew attention to this attitude as one needing change.

Second, widespread price cutting and competitive debasement reduced profit margins to a level which made re-equipment impossible. Furthermore the weavers, faced with a buyers' market for their output, tended to introduce innumerable small variations into their cloth, thereby shortening production runs and reducing the productivity of both machines and labour.[3]

Third was the generally negative attitude of producers towards re-equipment. Given their economic situation, this was hardly surprising. Observation suggested to them that the firms with the heaviest interest charges suffered most during slumps, and that the best chance of survival was to operate fully written-off machinery when there was a demand for goods, and close down the plant altogether at other times.

Fourth, such attempts as had been made to deal with the problems of redundant plant and price cutting were sectional, and furthermore often foundered because of the refusal of firms to co-operate. The Spindles Board, established by Act of Parliament in 1936, had scrapped 6 million spindles by 1939, 13 per cent of the number installed in 1935, but no similar arrangements were made for the weaving sector—though the number of looms did in fact decline—or for the finishing sector, though in this sector the principal firms involved did agree on some reduction of capacity. But various attempts to fix prices, regulate supplies by quotas, and carve up markets were not on the whole successful, as it proved impossible to get full co-operation from the numerous small firms engaged in the industry.

On the basis of this analysis, the Working Party concluded that there were four main issues before the industry:

(i)   the changed labour position—

[1] Board of Trade, *op. cit.* p. v.
[2] *ibid.* p. 8.
[3] For some examples of the number of variations that a single small weaver was prepared to produce, see chapter 4, p. 68.

'How can the industry which, up to 1939, relied on an over-plentiful highly skilled low-paid labour force, produce successfully and at competitive prices when it has to work with a limited, highly-paid labour force?';[1]

(ii)   the need to rationalize capacity;

(iii) the need to set up machinery for effective joint action by the industry;

(iv)   the problem of co-operation between industry and government.

It also drew attention to the problems and possibilities raised by scientific advances and the development of synthetics, and to the perhaps unpredictable but inevitable changes in external conditions as more countries established textile industries. In subsequent chapters of its Report, the Working Party analyzed in detail the structure of the industry, the labour position, the industry's existing plant and the problems of re-equipment, and the system of distribution. Its findings on the question of re-equipment are worth describing in more detail.

The Working Party based its assessment of the equipment position as it existed in 1945 on the findings of the Platt Mission, already described. A special sub-committee was appointed to investigate the question of re-equipment in relation to working costs. Its task was to investigate costs and costing methods with particular reference to :

(i)   what savings in cost could be achieved through longer runs (without changes in equipment);

(ii)   how costs of production would be affected by the installation of machinery efficiently used;

(iii) whether standard costing methods could be evolved to provide an index of efficiency and to provide a base for price policies.[2]

The sub-committee found that no comprehensive and reliable cost records were available within the industry. It suggested that an important first step was to draw up a uniform costing system for each section to which all firms could adhere, thereby making it possible to pool information on costs without revealing the identity of individual firms.

In an attempt to assess the possible benefits of re-equipment, the sub-committee calculated the costs of producing six different types of cloth, using five different combinations of equipment and working time. It took as a standard the costs of producing the cloths from yarn spun on mule spindles and woven on Lancashire (non-automatic) looms with a labour ratio of 4 looms per operative, all departments working with a single 48 hours shift per week. This method of production had already been found to be completely out-of-date by the Platt Mission, but it was nevertheless the prevailing technique at the time. Production costs

---

[1] Board of Trade, *op. cit.* p. 14.
[2] Board of Trade, *op. cit.* p. 67.

using the standard method were compared with the costs of producing the cloths from yarn produced by a high-draft ring spinning process, and woven on Lancashire looms with a labour ratio of 8 looms per operative or on automatic looms, with, for each type of loom, either a single shift of 48 hours per week or two shifts of 40 hours each per week.

The calculations were based on the following assumptions:

(a) *Wages*

The calculations were based on actual wage costs (as supplied by co-operating firms) rather than published wage rates and assumed that cost per shift for two shift working would be the same as for single shift working, i.e., a 20 per cent increase in hourly earnings.

(b) *Machinery and capital costs*

All the calculations included an element for capital costs, based on the then current value of new equipment of the type specified depreciated by the straight line method over 20 years for single shift working, 15 years for double shift working. Buildings were included at their 1939 values, depreciated over 50 years. Interest costs were also included at a rate of 5 per cent full replacement value of fixed stock plus 5 per cent of average working capital.[1]

(c) *Work per operative*

Even for the most 'modern' of the alternative techniques chosen, high-draft spinning and double-shift weaving on automatic looms, the labour saving envisaged was nothing like the levels that the Platt Mission had indicated were possible. In weaving, for example, the number of looms that a weaver could supervise was assumed to be between 12 and 20, according to the type of cloth, while the Platt Mission had found that American mills worked on a ratio of from 32 to as many as 60 looms per weaver.

On the basis of these assumptions, the savings to be expected from re-equipment were not very large. In no case was the saving on total conversion costs more than 10 per cent, with, in general, the savings from two shift working being the most important factor. It must also be remembered that these comparisons were all made against the costs of a typical Lancashire mill (mule spindles, 4 Lancashire looms per weaver)

[1] The deficiencies of these assumptions as providing an adequate guide to capital costs will be obvious. The Sub-committee's full thoughts on the matter (pp. 251–2 of the Report) are indicative of much confusion—'the rates we have used do not necessarily represent our views as to the proper level of capital charges to include in prices, which normally depend on market conditions as well as upon the necessity of prudent provision for eventual re-equipment and upon the remuneration of shareholders . . . As we are dealing with costs we would have preferred to avoid all reference to interest on capital employed . . .'

including the full replacement costs of such a plant, although in fact a large proportion of the mills of this type were operating with machinery that had long ago been written off. Thus any firm working fully depreciated machinery that looked at these calculations as an indication of the possible benefit of re-equipment might reasonably have concluded that the potential savings were negligible.

Although the Working Party's analysis of the situation and prospects of the cotton industry was presented as an agreed document, some of its more important recommendations were not unanimously supported. The main line of argument leading up to the recommendations was clear and logical. It started from the facts of the existing shortage of labour in relation to machine capacity and to the probable level of demand, and drew the primary conclusion that the industry would have to pay higher wages and offer improved working conditions in order to attract the labour force it wanted. The next step in the argument was to point out that high wages meant re-equipment in order to increase output per man hour and keep wage costs per unit of output down, and a further step, that the capital cost of re-equipment could only be financed on the basis of 'a large measure of two-shift working.'[1] The introduction of double shift working, combined with a change to high-draft ring spinning and weaving on automatic looms, would however mean a major reduction in the actual volume of equipment needed. The change from a one-shift 48 hour week to a two-shift 40 hour week, for example, would reduce the number of spindles required by 40 per cent, while a shift from mule to ring spindles would lead to a further reduction of 33 per cent. The final, and most important, step in the argument was the conclusion that the sort of fundamental transformation of the industry envisaged by the Working Party required joint action.

Following this analysis of the nature of the problem, the Working Party's main recommendations concerned consolidation (i.e. scrapping of plant) and re-equipment. The object of these recommendations was to provide the framework for a planned re-equipment programme. The main elements of this plan were:

(i) A proposal to accumulate a re-equipment fund within the industry by imposing a levy on producers, to be balanced by a corresponding increase in the controlled prices for yarn and cloth.

(ii) To create conditions under which the textile machinery industry could embark on a planned programme of expansion.

(iii) To create a balance between plant capacity and the available supply of labour.

---

[1] Board of Trade, *op. cit.* p. 163.

To these ends the Working Party proposed, besides the re-equipment levy, that a survey of existing machinery should be made, that an independent investigation of the textile machinery industry should be undertaken, and that plans should be made for the immobilization of some existing equipment.[1] Most significantly, the Working Party proposed that the different sections of the industry should be asked to work out detailed plans within a given period of time—three months was suggested. Some of those who signed the Report remembered the way in which the industry had drifted into stagnation and decline after 1918, and were determined that it should not happen again:

'One thing that must be done is that the unique opportunity of the short transition period of intensive demand should be used by the industry to get itself into shape to pay higher wages and to meet the difficult competitive conditions which lie ahead. The one thing that must be avoided is the enjoyment of this period as a fool's paradise of easy profits at the end of which the industry, and all those who rely on it for employment, may find themselves in worse difficulties even than those of the inter-war years.'[2]

'There must be some plan for, or positive assurance of, concerted action for achieving the objectives which we have stated, based on a recognition by all individual interests in the industry of an obligation to collaborate in joint action aimed at the maximum benefit for the industry as a whole.'[3]

It was this last proposition, and the course of action that it indicated, that led to a lengthy Memorandum of Dissent from the manufacturing and academic members of the Working Party. Their underlying doctrinal attitude was that 'free enterprise means free enterprise' and that management decisions were best left to individual businessmen. But their specific objections were mainly derived from their essentially short-term view of the nature of the problem. Noting that a sellers' market existed, they proposed the decontrol of export prices, in order to maximize export earnings, though they accepted the need for controlled domestic prices. And they opposed both large-scale re-equipment and enforced consolidation schemes, partly because of their attachment to free-enterprise principles, partly because of the need to avoid disruption of production, and partly because, they argued, traditional Lancashire equipment had certain technical advantages. They also suggested that the price of

---

[1] Mills closed under wartime concentration measures had been re-opened rapidly, and by the time the Working Party was finishing its report it calculated that only about 10 per cent of the total spindles in existence were in closed mills. There was therefore a need for fresh measures of consolidation.

[2] Board of Trade, *op. cit.* p. 164.

[3] *ibid.* p. 168.

textile machinery was 'probably much higher than it will be a few years hence,'[1] and they did not accept the fundamental premise of a continuing shortage of labour.

In the event, few of the Working Party's recommendations were carried out. The short-term view that had been emphasized so strongly by the dissentients prevailed, and although there was some decline in capacity and some re-equipment (see the next section of this chapter), there was no reorganization on the scale that the Working Party had envisaged. The closing paragraphs of the report were indeed prophetic of what was to come:

'. . . the tasks of readjustment with which the industry is confronted are of such a magnitude that they cannot be satisfactorily handled by the scattered efforts of individual units, and we cannot agree with those who argue that all that is needed now is to leave matters alone. We believe that such a course might lead now, as it did in the inter-war years, to economic loss and unsatisfactory human conditions of a kind which the nation cannot afford. The fact that the problems of readjustment now confronting the industry are in their nature totally different from those of the inter-war years does not alter this conclusion . . . we must once more emphasize our acute sense of the national need and of the greatness of the present opportunity for the cotton industry. If that opportunity is missed, its future is indeed likely to be "bound in shallows and in miseries".'[2]

4. THE POST-WAR BOOM, 1946–51

Between 1946 and 1951 the industry experienced the most sustained boom it had known during the century. Yarn production increased by 50 per cent and woven cloth production by 56 per cent. The spinning labour force increased by the same percentage as yarn production, while the weaving labour force rose by 51 per cent. Robson suggested that the small rise in productivity in weaving indicated by these figures could be accounted for partly by the increased use of rayon (which needs less work to prepare for weaving) and partly, perhaps, by the increasing use of automatic looms.[3]

Up to 1949 this boom reflected the world shortage of cotton goods. British export order books were full, despite the fact that by 1949 the unit value of printed cotton cloth for export was 79 per cent higher than the unit value of comparable United States exports. But British prices, though high, were not out of line with those of other European countries.

---

[1] Board of Trade, *op. cit.* p. 244.
[2] *ibid.* pp. 212–3.
[3] Robson, *op. cit.* p. 249.

By the end of 1949, however, world production had recovered to its 1936-8 level, and Japan and Western Europe were re-emerging as major exporters. In addition, the United States continued to maintain its exports at a much higher level than before the war.

By 1951 world exports of cotton textiles had recovered to 89 per cent of their pre-war (1936-8) level. But Britain's share of this trade had fallen from 27 per cent to 15 per cent. The decline would probably have been sharper but for three factors: devaluation, the liberalization of trade among western European countries from 1950 onwards and the impact of the Korean war. Domestic demand was strong up to the collapse of 1951.

What were the production policies of firms during this boom? Most firms took the simplest course open to them. They concentrated on recruiting an adequate labour force to operate as much as possible of their existing capacity, without making any major changes in organization or working methods. Although new wage 'lists', representing a considerable stepping-up of piece-work standards on which wages are based, were negotiated in 1949, they were not widely applied in individual mills. It has been estimated that in 1955, six years after the new system had been agreed, 90 per cent of weavers were still paid on the old system, though there was a limited acceptance of a 'more looms per weaver' policy.[1,2]

Despite the expansion in production and in the labour force available, there was a significant decline in the volume of machinery installed. In the spinning sector, the number of mule spindles fell from 23.1 million in 1945 to 17.7 million in 1951, a decline of over 23 per cent, while the number of ring spindles stayed approximately constant at 10.5 million. However since the new spindles installed, at a rate of 300,000 a year, were all ring, by 1951 17 per cent of ring spinning capacity, and about 8 per cent of total spinning capacity, was of post-war vintage. Over the same period the number of looms fell from 480,000 to 385,000—about 20 per cent—while the rate of installation of new looms averaged only 1,000 Lancashire and 3,000 automatic a year. Thus of the weaving capacity installed at the end of 1951 only 6 per cent was of post-war vintage, and only just over 10 per cent of the looms were automatic. The generally low rate of reinvestment can probably be attributed partly to 'short term' views that have already been described, and partly to the fact that the shortage of labour had turned out to be less acute than originally anticipated.

[1] H. A. Turner, *Trade Union Growth, Structure and Policy, a Comparative Study of the Cotton Unions* (George Allen & Unwin, 1962) p. 324.

[2] According to Robson, the favourable effects on labour productivity to be expected from this policy were largely offset from the labour usage point of view—though not from the point of view of total labour costs—by the higher proportion of lower paid ancillary workers required (*op. cit.* p. 249).

D

The rate of investment in spinning, expressed as a ratio of new units to units installed, was considerably higher than in weaving, and two factors may account for this. The first is the Cotton Spinning (Re-equipment Subsidy) Act of 1948, which authorized the payment of grants to the value of 25 per cent of re-equipment costs to groups of firms above a certain minimum size on condition that they closed down some of their mills while modernizing others. Although the Act was judged a failure, in that it failed to bring about concentration on the scale hoped for, nevertheless subsidies of £2.6 million on total re-equipment expenditure of £10 million were paid out. The Act may therefore have encouraged some re-equipment that might not otherwise have taken place.

A second factor was the shortage of textile machinery, which was acutely felt throughout the industry but may possibly have created even greater problems in the weaving sector than in the spinning sector. The Board of Trade Working Party's findings on the non-existence of an adequate supply of automatic looms have already been quoted, and furthermore it does seem that the sector of the textile machinery industry producing equipment for the spinning sector has historically tended to be both more technically advanced and of greater capacity than that producing looms and other equipment needed for weaving, at least during the last fifty years or more.

5. THE DECLINE, 1952–8

The year 1951 was a post-war peak for output, employment and exports. Between 1951 and 1952 yarn output fell by 28 per cent, cloth output by 27 per cent, and employment in the spinning and weaving sections by 21 and 16 per cent respectively. The reasons for the rapid increase in domestic consumption in 1950–1, and the severity of the subsequent slump, have been analysed in detail in an article by H. A. Turner and Roland Smith.[1] In brief, they found that the main reason for the rise in expenditure on clothing was the rise in real wages, and that the reasons for the slump were (i) the declining income-elasticity of demand for clothing, (ii) an irreversible shift to other forms of consumption, notably consumer durables which were just beginning to come on to the market in 1950, and (iii) the effects of the disproportionate rise in the prices of textile products, which had been increasing about one-third faster than consumer prices in general since 1947.

In this last connection, the impact of the policies of the Yarn Spinners' Association on price levels may be considered. After the removal of official price controls early in 1949 the Yarn Spinners' Association, which

[1] 'The Slump in the Cotton Industry, 1952', *Bulletin of the Oxford Institute of Statistics*, April 1953.

had been formed in 1947 with 'the general object of protecting the interest of spinners and in particular the maintenance of satisfactory prices',[1] asked its members to regard the previous fixed margins as minimum margins and so effectively created minimum prices. These pricing arrangements continued until 1958, when the Restrictive Practices Court ordered that the scheme be ended on the grounds that:

(i) It was a detriment to the public—i.e. to those who buy cotton goods, not just those who buy yarn.

(ii) That it handicapped the export trade in cloth, as it effectively set a lower limit to cloth as well as yarn prices.

(iii) That it tended to lead to excess capacity.[2]

The Court made the point that the maintenance of the arrangement would have to be paid for nationally, not locally, and not just in the form of higher prices for cotton goods or the loss of exports :

'. . . we have in mind chiefly the waste of national resources in the form of excess capacity. So long as the scheme lasts, concentration of the industry will be postponed; it will not be until the excess capacity has been got rid of that the industry can be made into a more compact entity, a reorganization which we believe will ultimately be beneficial not merely to the nation and to the consuming public, but to the industry itself and those employed in it'.[3]

The changes in the volumes of exports and imports from 1950 onwards certainly support the view that the British industry was becoming increasingly uncompetitive. In connection with the movements of imports, it should perhaps be noted that apart from 1951, when the sharp rise reflected 'boom psychology' and also, perhaps, an actual physical shortage of supplies (unfortunately no stock figures are available), imports did not begin to rise significantly until 1956–7, and not really sharply until 1958–9. The difficulties encountered by the industry in the early 1950's cannot therefore be directly attributed to Asian competition on the domestic market, though of course the fall in exports reflected Asian and other competition in third markets.

6. THE STRUCTURE OF THE INDUSTRY IN 1959

Table 3.2 shows the structure of the industry in April 1959, immediately before the coming into effect of the 1959 Act, which resulted in the elimination of a large number of firms. The way in which this and the other structural tables have been built up is described in the Statistical

[1] Robson, op. cit. p. 226.

[2] This summary of the Court's findings is taken from an interesting article by Alister Sutherland—'The Restrictive Practices Court and Cotton Spinning', in the Journal of Industrial Economics, October 1959.

[3] Quoted in ibid. p. 66.

Table 3.2. The structure of the Cotton Industry in April 1959

Size range (employment)	0	1–500		500–1000		1001–2000		2001 and over		All sizes		Employment—thousands % total employ- ment in industry	Mean size of firm
	No. of firms	No. of firms	Employ- ment	No. of firms	Employ- ment	No. of firms	Employ- ment	No. of firms	Employ- ment	No. of firms	Employ- ment		
Single-process firms													
Spinners	2	67	16.1	13	9.0	2	2.4	2	5.9	86	33.4	13.9	389
% in range			48.1		27.0		7.2		17.7		100		
Waste Spinners	—	23	1.6	—	—	—	—	—	—	23	1.6	0.6	68
% in range			100								100		
Doublers	5	68	4.1	2	1.4	—	—	—	—	75	5.5	2.3	73
% in range			74.0		26.0						100		
Weavers	27	519	53.6	17	11.7	4	6.2	—	—	567	71.4	29.6	126
% in range			75.0		16.4		8.6				100		
Finishers	2	164	13.6	7	4.6	2	2.1	2	7.4	177	27.7	11.5	156
% in range			49.1		16.7		7.6		26.6		100		
All single-process firms	36	841	88.9	39	26.8	8	10.7	4	13.3	928	139.6	57.9	150
% in range			63.7		19.2		7.6		9.5		100		
Multi-process firms	1	14	4.1	18	13.1	8	12.2	17	71.8	58	101.3	42.1	1746
% in range			4.1		13.0		12.0		70.9		100		
Total, all firms	37	855	93.0	57	39.9	16	22.8	21	85.1	986	240.9	100	244
% in range			38.6		16.6		9.5		35.3		100		

Source : Statistical Appendix.

Appendix. However, some special features about this table require comment. First, a number of firms with zero employment are shown in the table. They are included because they were still registered with the Cotton Board as being in existence and owning machinery and equipment, and were therefore eligible to apply for scrapping grants under the terms of the 1959 Act. Second, a distinction is made in the table between single-process and multi-process firms. The Cotton Board in fact classified the firms in the industry into 27 different types and combinations, but in order to simplify presentation, these have been reduced to 6, five categories of single-process firms and one category of multi-process firms—those engaged in both spinning and weaving, with or without any of the other activities of waste spinning, doubling and finishing.[1]

It will be noted that the analysis is in terms of firms rather than by establishments. Were it based on the latter, the number and weight of small units would be very much larger: the proportion of employment in the whole textiles sector in establishments with between 11 and 499 employees was 71.0 per cent in 1961,[2] and many of the larger firms were composed of a number of relatively small establishments. In Combined English Mills, for example, the average number of employees per mill was only 284, although the total number of people employed by the firm was 3,983.[3]

This table draws attention to the relatively small size of the single-process firms, with the partial exception of the spinners, among whom the rationalization schemes of the 1930's and the Act of 1948 had produced a number of bigger groups. The mean size of the 58 multi-process firms, 1,746 employees, was more than 10 times as large as that of the 928 single-process firms, and the 6 per cent of multi-process firms accounted for 42.1 per cent of total employment.

Some evidence as to the effects of mergers and re-grouping on the structure of the industry between 1940 and 1959 can be obtained from data on sizes measured by machinery employed. In the spinning sector (see table 3.3), there was a marked fall in the proportion of spindles installed by firms in the middle-sized group (80,001–200,000 spindles) and a rise in the proportion installed by the larger firms (200,001 and over). The total number of firms halved, but the average number of spindles installed per firm rose by 24 per cent.

---

[1] For an explanation of the reasons for this categorization, see chapter 4 p. 56. There is a table showing the relationship between my classification and the Cotton Board's in the Statistical Appendix.

[2] *Annual Abstract of Statistics, 1966* (H.M.S.O.) p. 21.

[3] E. Cummins, *op. cit.* By mid-1966, after re-organization, the average number employed per mill had risen to 330.

Table 3.3.   *Sizes of spinning firms, 1940 and 1959, measured by number of spindles installed*

spindles—mule equivalent, millions

Size range[a] No. of spindles installed	No. of firms	1940 No. of spindles	% total spindles	No. of firms	1959 No. of spindles	% total spindles
1— 20,000	23	0.3	1	14	0.2	0.8
20,001— 40,000	38	1.0	3	18	0.5	2.1
40,001— 80,000	78	4.5	11	42	2.5	10.3
80,001— 200,000	110	13.0	33	41	4.6	19.0
200,001—1,000,000	26	7.1	18	22	7.6	31.4
1,000,001 and over	5	13.2	34	4	8.9	36.8
Total, all sizes	280	39.1	100	141	24.2	100.0

Sources : 1940 : *Board of Trade Working Party Report, op. cit.*
           1959 : Cotton Board.
[a] The choice of size ranges was dictated by the data available for 1940.

In the weaving sector, by contrast, the shift was mainly downwards, the proportion of looms installed in small firms (400 or fewer looms) rising from 18.8 per cent in 1940 to 24.4 per cent in 1959.

Table 3.4.   *Sizes of weaving firms, 1940 and 1959, measured by numbers of looms installed*

looms, thousands

Size range[a] No. of looms installed	No. of firms	1940 No. of looms	% total looms	No. of firms	1959 No. of looms	% total looms
1— 200	438	38	7.6	315	28	11.4
201— 400	194	56	11.2	109	32	13.0
401— 800	253	146	29.2	107	61	24.8
801—2000	153	177	35.4	62	72	29.3
2001 and over	25	83	16.6	18	53	21.5
Total all sizes	1,063	500	100	611	246	100

Sources : 1940 : *Board of Trade Working Party Report.*
           1959 : Cotton Board.
[a] The choice of size ranges was dictated by the data available for 1940.

There was also an increase in the weight of large firms (2,001 or more looms) from 16.6 per cent of the total to 21.5 per cent. But the average number of looms installed per firm fell by 14.3 per cent.

Throughout the discussions leading up to the passage of the 1959 Act great stress was laid on the weakness of the weaving sector, with its large number of small weak firms, and the corresponding lack of integration between spinning and weaving operations.[1] This is borne out by the statistical evidence, which shows that the multi-process firms controlled

[1] Some of the technological implications of a largely horizontal structure have been discussed in chapter 2, and the changes in structure between 1959 and 1965 are analysed in chapter 6.

61.2 per cent of spinning spindles, 37.7 per cent of doubling spindles, and only 29.6 per cent of looms. These percentages must be interpreted somewhat cautiously, as the figures from which they are derived include shut down plant, though how much, in each section, is unknown except as a rough approximation. More important than the overall percentages of shut down plant, however, is its distribution between different types of firms. It may have been the case, for instance, though it is impossible to be sure, that the multi-process firms had a smaller proportion of shut down plant than did the single-process firms, and it may also have been the case that the shut down plant was differently distributed in different sectors.

CHAPTER 4

THE 1959 COTTON INDUSTRY ACT

Some earlier official attempts to promote rationalization and a faster rate of technical progress in the cotton industry have been described in the previous chapter. The present chapter is concerned with the 1959 Cotton Industry Act, which went considerably beyond any of them in aims and scope, and which indeed marked a new departure in the relationship between government and a privately owned industry in this country. The aims of the 1959 Act are discussed in the first part of the chapter, and its provisions in relation to its aims in the second part. The third part analyses the results of the Act. An attempt to form a judgement as to the success of the Act in achieving its aims, with comments on some special features, is deferred to the next chapter.

1. THE AIMS OF THE ACT

The background to the government's legislative proposals was given in a White Paper[1] that accompanied the publication of the Cotton Industry Bill in April 1959. These proposals originated with a speech by the Prime Minister, Mr. Harold Macmillan, to the Cotton Board Conference at Harrogate in October 1958. He said that if the industry could work out a plan for its own reorganization the government would give its most sympathetic attention to any ideas put forward, and made it clear that this included ideas that involved a measure of government financial assistance.

The government's motives were no doubt mixed.[2] But on the fundamental question as to whether the industry should be protected from external market forces, more particularly from imports from the developing countries of the Commonwealth, or should be encouraged to remodel itself in a way that would enable it to stand up to these forces, it took a clear, sensible and moderately courageous line. It recognized the importance of pursuing 'liberal economic policies towards the younger countries of the emerging continents', as well as the undesirability of

---

[1] Board of Trade, *Reorganization of the Cotton Industry*, Cmnd. 744 (1959).

[2] The timing of the measures in relation to political events cannot be ignored. At a by-election held in Rochdale in February 1958, there was a swing of 13.6 per cent to Labour, the largest swing against the government in any by-election between 1955 and 1959, though helped by a Liberal intervention, and the government had to face a general election by the spring of 1960 at the latest (see Butler and Rose, *The British General Election of 1959*, (Macmillan, 1960) Appendix VI, p. 283.

upsetting the Commonwealth Preference System by introducing tariffs on cotton goods, and further stated that it was not prepared to impose quantitative restrictions on cotton goods beyond the 'voluntary limitations' on exports agreed between the United Kingdom cotton industry and the industries of Hong Kong, India, and Pakistan.

In other circumstances than those that prevailed in Lancashire in 1959, such a stand might have been more than moderately courageous. An industry struggling to survive does not readily let a government get away with proposals involving a relatively liberal import policy. But the cotton industry, although strongly organized through its trade associations, and, in addition, well represented politically, recognized that the decline had gone too far to be arrested by protection alone. The main cause of the long contraction since the 1920's, it is worth recalling, was the loss of export markets, including the re-export trade, and not the flow of imports into the British market, and it was falling exports that had produced the conditions of surplus capacity and an ill-adapted production and marketing structure that were the problems the industry faced in the 1950's. So the industry seized on the Prime Minister's offer, and in November the Cotton Board set up a special Development Committee to consider what might best be done. By January 1959 this committee, which was made up of representatives of the main sections of the industry— spinners, weavers, finishers, and merchants—and the trade unions, had drawn up provisional estimates of surplus plant, and had started discussions with the government. From these discussions emerged, another three months later, the White Paper and the Bill.

Not the least of the remarkable features of the 1959 Act is the extent to which the government depended on the industry, working through its trade associations and the Cotton Board, to draw up the general framework and many of the details of the legislation to be enacted in its favour. There was no preliminary official committee of enquiry into the factual background, or into the need for specific measures, nor was there any attempt, at least in public, to consider the relative merits of various possible alternative measures in the light of expert opinion and evidence. One reason for making such a hasty assault on the problem was the need for speed in bringing actual measures into operation, partly because of the limited 'breathing space' for readjustment provided by the voluntary limitation on imports and partly because of the need to force through contraction in a short time once the idea of a special scheme had been introduced. People in the industry felt that one reason why earlier plans for contraction had failed was because they were spread over too long a period, encouraging firms to wait and see what their competitors did before deciding whether to scrap or not themselves, and were determined to ensure that there should be the minimum time allowed for the whole process on this occasion. A second reason was, no doubt, that extensive enquiries into the cotton industry's plight had already been made,[1] and furthermore that the main source of statistical information about the machinery position was the data collected by the Cotton Board's statistical department, much of it for publication. The existence of this source of data was one of the achievements of the Board of Trade Working Party. Political expediency may have been a third reason.

This hurried and one-sided approach to the industry's problems helps to explain the generally weak and under-argued case for the proposals given in the White Paper, despite its fundamentally clear perception of the need for contraction and reorganization, and its recognition of the fact that some sort of a push was needed to accelerate the speed of re-adjustment. The estimates of surplus capacity, to start with, give no precise impression of the nature of the problem, chiefly because they are not related to any concept or definition of capacity. 'Capacity' is a fluid quantity that needs precise definition in a given context, in terms of 'normal' output, 'normal' working hours per machine, and 'normal' machine/labour ratios. In the calculations presented in the White Paper 'surplus capacity' seems to have been the sum of completely idle equipment plus a proportion of partly used equipment, based, one can only deduce, on single-shift working for machines and men as the norm.

The object of the Act, as described in the White Paper, was 'to bring about a reorganized and re-equipped industry which could compete with success in the markets of the world with the types of cloth that are wanted wherever living standards are high'. It proposed to do this by first reducing the size of the industry, in terms of the physical plant employed, by a minimum of 50 per cent in spinning and about 40 per cent in weaving and finishing, and then by encouraging the remaining firms to re-equip. The way in which these proposals were implemented, and some other administrative aspects of the Act, are discussed in the next section. But one further important point about the general nature of the Act needs to be made. It is that none of the measures proposed were in any way linked to a preconceived idea of an appropriate structure for the industry. There was no lower limit to the size of grants for either scrapping or re-equipment, and no attempt to limit eligibility to firms of a certain minimum size, as had been the case in the 1948 Cotton Spinning (Re-equipment) Act for example. Nor was there any pressure towards a more vertical structure for the industry. This completely neutral view is the more surprising in that the various earlier studies of the industry referred to in the previous chapter all emphasized the need for structural changes, though they were certainly far from unanimous as to whether

[1] Two of these enquiries, the Platt Mission of 1944 and the Board of Trade Working Party of 1945, were discussed in chapter 3.

a more vertical structure or a more concentrated horizontal structure was needed. The Platt Mission, for instance, had suggested that productivity in yarn preparation and weaving could never increase fast unless there was more vertical integration, while the Board of Trade Working Party favoured both greater horizontal concentration and a more vertical structure.

However, in the absence of any serious analysis of the true state of the cotton industry and the nature of its problems, it may have been just as well that the Act did not attempt to impose a structure on the industry. It would probably have been an inappropriate one. Only since the passage of the Act, as we shall see in the next chapter, has the scale of the new thinking and action required to create an appropriate structure for the textile industry become apparent.

It is interesting to compare the very different approach to rationalization adopted by the government more recently in tackling the problems of the shipbuilding industry. Recognizing that uninformed action was unlikely to be effective, in 1965 it set up a special committee of enquiry, the members of which were mainly drawn from outside the industry, to 'establish what changes are necessary in organization, in the methods of production, and in any other factors affecting costs, to make the shipbuilding industry competitive in world markets ; to establish what changes in organization and methods of production would reduce costs of manufacture of large main engines of ships to the lowest level ; and to recommend what action should be taken by employers, trade unions and the Government, to bring about these changes'.[1] The Committee asked itself some fundamental questions: 'Why should Britain continue to build a lot of ships?' (p. 8); 'Will all the effort (of reorganization) be worthwhile, or would the resources be better transferred to something else?' (p. 11); 'How can competitiveness be regained?' (p. 9); and took a year to produce a Report of 200 pages, including extensive technical analysis of the industry's problems. It suggested a framework for reorganization, and proposed mergers, with financial assistance, along the lines now being urged on the industry by the Industrial Reorganization Corporation.

2. THE ADMINISTRATIVE PROVISIONS OF THE ACT

The object of the 1959 Act, as we have seen, was to bring about the contraction and reorganization of the cotton industry by subsidizing the scrapping of obsolete plant and assisting re-equipment in the remaining mills. The way in which the government gave effect to its proposals to encourage scrapping and re-equipment is described in the following paragraphs. General discussion of the validity of the Act's approach

---

[1] *Shipbuilding Inquiry Committee 1965–66 Report*, Cmnd. 2937 (1966).

to the problems of the industry, and the success of the measures in furthering its aims, is reserved for the next chapter.

Pressure for financial assistance for re-equipment seems to have come from the industry. The government had originally planned to limit its financial assistance to grants for firms scrapping equipment, but the industry, which was primarily concerned with the import problem, felt that a promise to assist re-equipment would amount to an implicit guarantee about imports. It reasoned that a government that had given money for re-equipment would provide protection from disruptive imports while reorganization plans were being worked out and put into operation—a process that must be expected to take several years.[1] The government agreed to give financial assistance for re-equipment, but stipulated that no re-equipment grants would be forthcoming until a specified proportion of existing capacity had been eliminated: implementation of the Act thus fell into two distinct parts, which will be described separately.

(a) *The scrapping schemes*[2]

It has earlier been suggested that the scrapping provisions of the Act went considerably beyond any previous governmental attempt to encourage the reorganization of a privately owned industry. Most notably, they included direct financial assistance towards the elimination of surplus capacity. The main features of the scrapping schemes were first, that they were voluntary and automatic; second, that the government bore two-thirds of the total cost of buying up machinery to be scrapped; and third, that specific provisions were made for people losing their jobs as a result of concentration.

First we may consider the sense in which participation in the schemes was voluntary, and compensation paid automatically. The arrangements made for scrapping in the spinning, doubling and weaving sectors were published in July 1959. Under them, any firm active in the appropriate section of the industry could offer equipment of certain named kinds for scrapping. Provided that this equipment met the basic criterion of eligibility—that it was in working order (whether or not it was actually running) or could be put into working order easily and cheaply—the firm automatically received compensation at a fixed rate per spindle or loom. The standard rates were, for spinning, 8 shillings per mule equivalent spindle and £250 per carding engine, for doubling, 10–14 shillings per spindle, depending on the type, and for weaving, £60–£80 per loom, depending on the width of the loom. These standard rates applied to working machinery scrapped by firms staying in the industry; they were

---

[1] For a discussion of the imports question, see chapter 6.

[2] The official euphemism was 're-organization' schemes. But that was precisely what they were not. I have referred to them as scrapping schemes throughout.

increased by 25 per cent for machinery scrapped by firms leaving the industry altogether, and reduced by 25 per cent for idle machinery and machinery in closed mills. There were thus three rates of compensation: the premium rate, for firms leaving the industry, and the standard and discount rates, for firms scrapping only part of their equipment, and staying in business themselves. The analysis of the results of these schemes that follows in part 3 of this chapter distinguishes between 'premium rate' and 'other' firms according to the rate of compensation received.

The specifications of eligible types of equipment referred only to function, not to date of manufacture or potential productive capacity. In order to get paid, firms scrapping machinery had to prove that it had been physically destroyed: however, firms with some machinery having a second-hand value higher than the scrapping price could sell it, given official approval for the sale, and still be eligible for compensation for the rest of their plant. A further aspect of the 'automatic' nature of the schemes was their applicability to all firms in the industry, that is to all firms that met the Cotton Board's criteria, without reference to their geographical situation. No attempt was made, by varying the rates or by deliberate selection of mills to be closed down, to prevent closures in areas with few other employment opportunities.

For the schemes to come into operation at all, a minimum amount of machinery had to be offered for scrapping in each section. And because speed was thought to be very important, for reasons mentioned already, firms were only given two months, August and September 1959, to make up their minds about scrapping. They were even offered a bonus of 5 per cent for making their applications before the end of August. Had an insufficient amount of machinery been offered for scrapping, taking into account probable sales and probable ineligible equipment, the Board could have refused to pay any compensation to the section affected, but the problem did not arise.

The schemes for the yarn and cloth finishing sections of the industry, though similar in principle to the spinning, doubling and weaving schemes, differed somewhat owing to the lack of a convenient unit of capacity. This meant that some other basis for calculating compensation had to be found: the method used was to take both the value of the equipment being scrapped and the size of the firm's turnover into account—50 per cent of the written-down value of plant and machinery was added to 15 per cent of turnover in the firm's financial year ending not later than 31st October, 1959. It also meant that in order to qualify firms had to close down whole plants rather than just scrapping some machinery within a plant.

Working out a suitable formula took some time, and the finishing schemes were not introduced until August 1960. Then firms were given a rather longer period to make up their minds than spinning, doubling and weaving firms had been allowed, extending to January 1961. As with the earlier schemes, the Board of Trade set minima for the proportion of capacity to be eliminated in each of the main sub-sections of woven cloth finishing—bleaching, dyeing and printing—and for yarn processing. These minima were all exceeded, and the actual process of scrapping began in the spring of 1961.[1]

Two-thirds of the compensation payable to firms scrapping machinery came from the government, with the other third, together with costs of administration, being raised by a levy on firms in the relevant section. This policy was a considerable departure from that adopted for earlier rationalization schemes, including cotton spinning in 1936–39, when government participation was limited to financial guarantees and loan facilities. The 1936 Spindles Board was permitted to raise money by issuing guaranteed debenture stock, in order to bridge the gap in time between its purchases for scrapping, which were spread over three years, and the redemption of costs through levies, which was spread over fifteen years. But the actual costs of buying up and scrapping spindles were wholly met by a levy on spinning firms.

A third innovation in the Act was the requirement that provision be made for the compensation of employees who lost their jobs as a result of scrapping, or, indeed, as a result of re-equipment. The terms of compensation were not fixed by the government, but left to negotiation between trade associations and unions, the government reserving the right to withhold payment of grants unless satisfactory arrangements were made. A memorandum setting out the agreed scales and methods of payment was published in July 1959.[2] Once again, there were certain important automatic features about these payments. They were based solely on age (subject to a minimum total length of service in the industry of 5 years since 1945), and were related to average weekly earnings. Thus ano perative aged 27–29 was entitled to three weeks' earnings, and an operative aged 65 or more to 30 weeks' earnings.[3] Half the entitlement was payable as a lump sum: the other half was spread over a number of weeks, with downward adjustments if the worker got another job. The

[1] Full details of all the schemes will be found in the following Statutory Instruments : spinning, S.I. 1959 No. 1325 ; doubling, S.I. 1959 No. 1324 ; weaving, S.I. 1959 No. 1326 ; yarn processing, S.I. 1960 No. 1265 ; and woven cloth finishing, S.I. 1960 No. 1264.

[2] There were in fact two separate agreements, one for spinning, doubling and weaving and the other for finishing.

[3] This wage-related compensation system applied to operatives in the spinning, doubling and weaving sectors. Operatives in the finishing sector got a fixed payment per year of work, rising with the total number of years worked. Lower rates per year worked were paid to women.

payments were financed entirely by levies on firms in the relevant section of the industry.

One further unusual feature of the scrapping provisions of the Act must be described. It is the way in which the schemes were administered. This job was carried out by the Cotton Board, which was responsible for making sure that machinery and plant offered for scrapping had in fact been physically destroyed, that any employees affected were receiving the compensation to which they were entitled, and that, for premium rate firms, each firm applying had in fact ceased operations in any part of the industry. Had the Cotton Board not existed, it would have been impossible to carry out rationalization schemes of the kind that have been described. In the first place, the Board possessed detailed knowledge of the amounts and kinds of machinery installed in particular mills, by virtue of its statutory duty to collect such information compulsorily from all firms in the industry. It also had an accumulated store of information about the financial relationships and structure of the many individual firms—nearly 1,000—eligible to participate in the schemes. This was invaluable when it came to deciding which firms were eligible for compensation at premium rates. Furthermore the Board was technically competent to determine whether or not the machinery met the basic criterion—whether, if idle, it could be put into working order quickly and cheaply, and whether it was suitable for, and used for, processing the types of fibres specified under the Act.

In its administration of the schemes, the Cotton Board acted as more than the agent of the government. It had full executive powers, including the power to determine the distribution of public money, which was paid to firms by the Cotton Board and not by the Board of Trade. Furthermore, if a firm wanted to dispute a settlement with the Cotton Board, it had to take the Board to court. The Board of Trade was powerless to intervene.[1]

(b) The Re-equipment schemes

The administrative details of the re-equipment schemes included no important novel features, and require less detailed description. The Cotton Board was for this purpose appointed as an agent of the Board of Trade, which kept to itself the responsibility for paying out grants on the basis of recommendations put forward by the Cotton Board. The conditions under which a firm was eligible for a grant were broadly defined. The firm had to submit evidence that the expenditure on which the grant was claimed was 'the whole or part of a considered scheme for

[1] See *House of Commons Fourth Report from the Estimates Committee, Session 1961–62, Assistance to the Cotton Industry,* (1962), pages 20–21. Detailed accounts of the administration of the schemes are given in memoranda by the Board of Trade and the Cotton Board published in this document.

re-equipping or modernizing a mill . . .', and the main categories of equipment for which grants could be obtained were all spinning, doubling and weaving equipment, including equipment needed for intermediate processes such as winding and yarn preparation, and all equipment used for yarn and cloth finishing. Second-hand equipment was not eligible, but modifications to existing equipment, such as automatic knotters and automatic loom attachments, were. So was imported machinery, and so, too, were items such as air-conditioning plant, lifts and mechanical conveyors and power plants, although buildings were excluded. A firm wanting to make improvements in several of its productive units had to make a separate claim in respect of each unit, and there was a lower limit of £2,500 per claim. There were also provisions for the refunding by firms of compensation received for scrapping if the new equipment was intended to *replace* the scrapped machinery. Such was the rate of decline, however, that these 'clawback' provisions were little used.

The timing of the whole re-equipment phase of the Act was spread over the years 1960–64. Firms in the spinning, doubling and weaving sections had to submit their applications for approval in principle by July 1962, place orders for new equipment by July 1963 (originally also July 1962), and complete the purchase and installation of this equipment by July 1964. The time-table for the finishing sections was the same, except that they were given until July 1963 to place their orders from the start. At every stage the progress of an approved scheme was supervized by the Cotton Board, an independent firm of accountants, and the Board of Trade's accountants, and the Cotton Board also examined its technical aspects.

3. THE RESULTS OF THE ACT

In analyzing the results of the Act, two separate questions require answering: first, what effects did it have on the structure of the industry, and second, how were the payments distributed. As the scrapping phase and re-equipment phase were fairly widely separated in point of time, and the industry had undergone considerable structural changes that were only in part a consequence of the Act before re-equipment was completed, it seems advisable to consider these two questions separately in relation to each of the two phases of the Act.

The compilation of the data on which this analysis is based is described in the Statistical Appendix. The main problem encountered was the choice of a suitable measure of size, and it is perhaps worth drawing attention to it here, since it does limit and qualify the conclusions that can be drawn from the data. Briefly, four alternative measures of size were considered. The first, size of assets, was quickly rejected in view of the large number of private companies in the industry for which no information on asset structure is available. In any case, the problem of turning companies' own data on their assets into a form providing a useful basis for comparative measurement would be a major one in an industry in which many firms have completely written off their plant, and make little or no provision for depreciation but which nevertheless continue to function. A second possible measure was volume of output, and this in some ways would have been a satisfactory one, though the difficulties of choosing an appropriate time period in an industry working very much below capacity would have been considerable. The major objection to output, however, was that no detailed information on the output of individual firms is available. A third possible measure, the amount of equipment installed, raised difficult problems when it came to the measurement of the size of vertically integrated firms. It is hard to see how varying quantities of spindles and looms in different firms could be added together to give a measure of the total size of each individual firm, and even if this could be done it would still leave out the various intermediate processes that are distributed among firms in a random way. Furthermore, a simple measure of equipment, such as numbers of spindles or looms installed, unweighted by any utilization factor, would give a misleading picture of the relative sizes of firms.

The fourth measure of size considered, and the one that was eventually chosen, was employment. Even this is by no means a perfect measure, and it is important to be clear about its limitations. The most significant of these is that the use of employment as a measure of size obscures both the dispersion of labour productivity among firms at a given point in time and shifts in productivity within individual firms when comparing the structure of the industry at two points in time. There is no systematic evidence for the industry as to dispersion of labour productivity among firms of different sizes, or even whether productivity is related to size, but the author's enquiries among firms of different sizes and types indicate that the larger firms do on the whole obtain higher rates of output per employee, particularly since about 1963, and that productivity has grown faster among big firms than among small. The data therefore tend to underestimate the weight of the larger firms in relation to their output and therefore to their share of the market.

A further limitation is that units of labour are not homogeneous. The Cotton Board data are for all employees on the books of a firm, from managers to young entrants, men and women, full-time and part-time workers. These last are uniformly counted as halves. In addition, firms in the same broad group, e.g., spinners or weavers, do not necessarily perform exactly the same range of activities. Some spinning firms, for example, may also prepare all or part of the yarn they produce for the

E

next process in the chain of textile manufacture—dyeing it, sizing it, making up bigger packages by winding it onto different bobbins, and so on, while other spinning firms undertake no further preparatory work.

In some of the tables that follow, firms have been classified into two main groups, 'single-process firms' and 'multi-process firms'. These headings have been used, rather than simply 'horizontal' and 'vertical' firms, because it does not necessarily follow from the fact that a firm was both a spinner and a weaver that it was a truly vertically organized enterprise. The links may have been solely financial. Firms in the first group have been further sub-divided into spinners, doublers, weavers and finishers. As doubling is not really a manufacturing process at all, but simply a form of yarn preparation (see chapter 2), spinner-doublers have been included with spinners, and weaver-doublers with weavers. This means that the distinguishing characteristic of the firms in the second group—the 'multi-process firms'—is that they were all engaged in both spinning and weaving. Some of them were also doublers and/or finishers.

(a) The scrapping phase

It will be recalled that under the reorganization provisions of the Act firms wanting to scrap equipment could apply for compensation at one of three rates, premium, standard or discount. The premium rate was for firms active in April 1959 that nevertheless intended to leave the industry altogether, the standard rate for firms scrapping part of their actively operating plant, while remaining in business, and the discount rate for firms scrapping idle plant. The immediate effects of the scrapping

Table 4.1. *Structure of the Lancashire textile industry, 1959, before and after elimination of 'premium rate' firms under the 1959 Act*

Type of firm and size range	Before 1959 Act		After 1959 Act		Number of firms leaving industry ('Premium rate' firms)
	No. of firms	% employment	No. of firms	% employment	
Single process firms					
0	36	—	30	—	6
1— 500	841	36.9	658	32.6	183
501—1000	39	11.1	32	10.3	7
1001 and over	12	9.9	12	11.2	—
Total	928	57.9	732	54.1	196
Multi-process firms					
0	1	—	1	—	—
1— 500	14	1.7	10	1.4	4
501—1000	18	5.5	15	5.1	3
1001 and over	25	34.9	25	39.4	—
Total	58	42.1	51	45.9	7
Total, all industry	986	100	783	100	203

Source : Statistical Appendix.

schemes on the structure of the industry were therefore to reduce the number of firms by those opting for premium rate compensation and leaving the industry altogether.

Table 4.1 summarizes the effects of the elimination of the premium rate firms on the structure of the industry. It will be seen that the firms closing down were all relatively small, with 1,000 or fewer employees, and that nearly all of them—97 per cent—were single-process firms. The net effect of their removal, assuming no change in the employment of the remaining firms, was thus to increase the weight of the multi-process firms in the industry, from 42 per cent of total employment to 46 per cent, and also to increase the weight of the larger firms. However, the most notable feature of this table, and one which requires closer analysis, is that under a quarter of the firms in the 1–500 group elected to leave the industry under the scheme, which was primarily directed at them.

Of the 841 single-process firms with between 1 and 500 employees in the industry in 1959, 658 (78 per cent) were weavers or finishers. The average size of the 519 weaving firms was about 103 employees, and of the 164 finishing firms, 83 employees. Table 4.2 analyzes these two

Table 4.2.   *Analysis of participation by small weaving and finishing firms in the scrapping schemes of the 1959 Act*

	Size range					Total
	1–100	101–200	201–300	301–400	401–500	1–500
Weavers						
Number of firms at April 1959	331	116	46	16	10	519
Employment, percentage	*100*	*100*	*100*	*100*	*100*	*100*
Number leaving industry	84	23	5	2	2	116
Employment, percentage	*26.0*	*19.5*	*9.9*	*12.1*	*20.4*	*18.6*
Number remaining, of which :—	247	93	41	14	8	403
(i) Number scrapping some plant	74	44	24	7	3	152
Employment, percentage	*24.4*	*37.6*	*53.5*	*46.0*	*29.8*	*37.4*
(ii) Number not participating in scheme	173	49	17	7	5	251
Employment, percentage	*49.6*	*42.9*	*36.6*	*36.6*	*49.8*	*44.0*
Finishers						
Number of firms at April 1959	120	30	7	4	3	164
Employment, percentage	*100*	*100*	*100*	*100*	*100*	*100*
Number leaving industry	20	6	1	—	—	27
Employment, percentage	*18.4*	*19.7*	*12.7*	—	—	*14.5*
Number remaining, of which :—	100	24	6	4	3	137
(i) Number scrapping some plant	3	2	1	—	—	6
Employment, percentage	*3.1*	*7.4*	*15.7*	—	—	*5.4*
(ii) Number not participating in scheme	97	22	5	4	3	131
Employment, percentage	*78.5*	*72.9*	*71.6*	*100*	*100*	*80.1*

Source : Statistical Appendix.

groups of small firms in more detail. It shows that 22 per cent of the weaving firms left the industry, and only 16 per cent of the finishing firms, with the largest proportion of leavers in both groups coming from the smallest firms. The percentage of employees affected was thus smaller than the percentage of firms: 18.6 per cent of those employed in the weaving sector and 14.5 per cent of those employed in the finishing sector were made redundant.

In the weaving sector, even in the group of firms with 1–100 employees, the smallest firms of all, only just over a quarter left the industry altogether, and a further 22 per cent scrapped some equipment. Over half the firms in this size-range took no part in the scheme. Among the whole 519 firms with 500 or fewer employees, 251 (48 per cent), accounting for 44 per cent of total employment, stayed outside the scheme altogether. For the finishing sector, the proportion of firms participating was even lower. Apart from the firms leaving the industry, only 6 others (4 per cent) scrapped some plant, these firms accounting for 5.4 per cent of total employment.

The horizontally organized doubling firms also responded poorly to the scheme, only 6 out of a possible 66 firms with 200 or less employees leaving the industry. The spinners, by contrast, took full advantage of it, 35 out of 69 (51 per cent) in the 500 or less group going out of business altogether, and 19 out of the remaining 34 scrapping some equipment.[1]

The most obvious reason that suggests itself for these differences in behaviour by the various sections of the industry is that the standard rates of payment per doubling spindle and per loom were fixed too low to induce firms to leave the industry. But this, while it may have been part of the reason, does not seem to have been the whole reason. The question of minimum scale of operations is relevant. Whereas there is an identifiable lower limit of size for spinning firms, determined partly by technical considerations and partly by the gain in efficiency achievable through long runs, there is not, or has not been until recently at any rate, a significant lower limit of size for a weaving firm, given prevailing techniques and organization. Where each loom works as an independent unit, weaving yarn that is bought in from other firms, there is no real barrier, given the technology practised by small firms, to running a business with 50 looms or less—perhaps 20 to 25 employees including the owner. In fact there were 92 weaving firms with 50 or fewer looms each in March 1959, and by March 1960 the number had only fallen by 17 per cent to 76 firms. The continued existence of many of these small firms has been and still is helped by the fact that they tend to be established in the more remote towns and villages where labour is less mobile, particularly the married women on whom they depend.

[1] See table S.A.2, page 120.

Nothing is known about the financial position of these small firms, and it is not possible to state categorically that they were completely inelastic to changes in the selling price of looms. But against this view should be recorded the attitude of one weaving firm visited by the author, which refused to take any part in the scheme, and said that it could not have been induced to sell out at any price, as it attached the greatest importance to remaining independent of the government whatever the circumstances.

The small number of finishing firms scrapping part of their plant can be accounted for by the administrative procedures of the scheme as it applied to them. It will be recalled that, owing to the absence of a convenient unit of equipment such as a spindle or loom, finishing firms wanting to scrap plant had to be prepared to close down a whole works and scrap everything in it. Obviously the smaller the firm, the more likely it was to have all its activities concentrated in one works, and so to be faced with the radical choice of closing down completely or making no changes. This explains why so few firms scrapped part of their plant, but it does not explain why only a relatively small proportion decided to leave the industry altogether. One important reason was the boom conditions prevailing at the time the scheme for finishing came into operation, the autumn of 1960. A second may have been the organization of the trade in converting imported grey cloth, which was being bought by merchants for converting and subsequent resale on home or foreign markets. The small finishing firms, ready to accept short runs or special orders, could expect to attract a large share of this business.

In the industry as a whole, 296 firms, accounting for 64 per cent of total employment, scrapped some equipment at standard or discount rates.[1] As table 4.3 shows, the multi-process firms participated in the schemes to a much greater extent than did the single-process firms, with only 3 firms accounting for 4.6 per cent employment in the former group remaining altogether outside the schemes compared with 484 firms accounting for 39.2 per cent of employment in the latter. The reasons for the low rate of participation among weavers and finishers have already been discussed. Much the same sort of reasons affected the doubling firms, with the additional factor that according to the Cotton Board's original estimates there was relatively little surplus capacity in the doubling sector to begin with. What is interesting is how few firms with activity in the spinning sector stayed outside the schemes, whether they were single-process firms or combined in some way with other activities.

What table 4.3 does not show is the effects of standard and discount rate scrapping on the structure of the industry. The employment data

---

[1] It is impossible to separate standard rate payments from discount rate payments, as many firms received payments at both rates, standard in respect of machinery running in April 1959 and discount in respect of machinery in closed mills.

provide a measure of the number and weight of firms involved in the schemes to some extent but do not give any indication of the actual changes in the productive capacity of firms, as measured by the amount of equipment installed, that resulted from scrapping. This is because the employment figures for standard and discount rate firms include all employment in a firm scrapping any equipment: among the 48 multi-process firms receiving compensation, 28 scrapped spindles and looms, 14 scrapped spindles only and 6 looms only.

Table 4.3. *Numbers and sizes of firms participating in 1959 Act scrapping, by type of firm*

| Type of firm | Total, all firms | Applicants | | Non-applicants |
| | | Premium rate | Standard and discount rate | |
	No. of firms	No. of firms	No. of firms	No. of firms
Single-process firms				
Spinners	86	36	33	17
Employment percentage	*100*	*24.5*	*33.3*	*22.2*
Waste spinners	23	—	—	23
Employment percentage	*100*	—	—	*100*
Doublers	75	7	20	48
Employment percentage	*100*	*5.7*	*32.1*	*62.2*
Weavers	567	123	183	261
Employment percentage	*100*	*17.3*	*42.2*	*40.5*
Finishers	177	30	12	135
Employment percentage	*100*	*12.7*	*38.8*	*48.5*
Total, single-process firms	928	196	248	484
Employment percentage	*100*	*17.5*	*43.3*	*39.2*
Multi-process firms	58	7	48	3
Employment percentage	*100*	*3.3*	*92.1*	*4.6*
Total, all firms	986	203	296	487
Employment percentage	*100*	*11.5*	*63.8*	*24.7*

Source : Statistical Appendix.

For an indication of changes in installed capacity one must turn to data on machinery scrapped. Table 4.4 gives details for premium rate firms, the rest, and the whole industry. One point about the premium rate figures calls for an explanation. It will be seen that except for the doublers, in no case did the amount of machinery scrapped equal the amount installed, although premium rate compensation was only payable to firms scrapping *all* plant. This discrepancy is mainly explained by machinery sales, permitted under the terms of the schemes, and also to a minor extent by the fact that a few of the looms installed were used for weaving ineligible fabrics, such as wool, and so were not themselves eligible for compensation payments.

In the whole industry 48 per cent of spindles installed at April 1959 were scrapped, compared with 27 per cent of doubling spindles and 38 per

Table 4.4. *Machinery scrapped under 1959 Act, by rate of premium paid and main types of firm*

Type of firm	Spinning Spindles			Doubling Spindles			Looms		
	Installed	Scrapped (millions)	% scrapped	Installed	Scrapped (thousands)	% scrapped	Installed	Scrapped (thousands)	% scrapped
Single-process firms									
Premium rate	2.9	2.6	89.7	172	172	99.8	57.7	55.7	96.5
Other	6.9	2.4	34.6	1,099	142	12.9	123.5	20.4	16.5
All equipment, single-process firms	9.8	5.0	51.0	1,272	314	24.7	181.2	76.0	41.9
Multi-process firms									
Premium rate	0.5	0.4	93.9	12	12	95.1	4.5	3.6	80.3
Other	13.8	6.7	44.8	758	219	28.8	71.8	18.2	25.3
All equipment, multi-process firms	15.4	7.1	46.3	770	230	29.9	76.2	21.8	28.6
All firms									
Premium rate	3.4	3.0	90.2	185	184	99.5	62.1	59.2	95.4
Other	21.8	9.1	41.6	1,857	361	19.4	195.3	38.6	19.7
All equipment	25.2	12.1	48.1	2,042	544	26.7	257.4	97.8	38.0
(Minimum required to scrap for scheme to operate)		6.0			400			45.0	

Source : Statistical Appendix.

cent of looms. The multi-process firms scrapped 40 per cent more spinning spindles than did the single-process firms, but in the doubling and weaving sectors the position was reversed, with the single-process firms scrapping 36 per cent more doubling spindles and nearly two and a half times as many looms as the multi-process firms. It seems that, in spinning, many of the big combines took the opportunity to scrap enormous numbers of mule spindles, many of them out of production and in closed mills. Over half of the total looms scrapped came from weaving firms leaving the industry, many of whom, in view of their small size, had no choice but to scrap everything or stay as they were.

To conclude this analysis of the results of the scrapping schemes, we may look at the distribution of compensation payments. As might be expected, since the payments were fixed at standard rates per spindle or loom, table 4.5 looks much the same as the other distributional tables, with the single-process firms receiving 91 per cent of the premium rate payments and the multi-process firms 62 per cent of the standard and discount rate payments. Taking both categories of payment together, the multi-process firms got 35 per cent of the total, the weavers 31 per cent and the spinners 25 per cent.

Table. 4.5. *Analysis of total scrapping compensation payments, by type of payment and type of firm*

Type of firm	Premium	Standard and Discount	£ thousands Total
Single-process firms			
Spinners	2,809	1,523	4,332
Percentage	*33.0*	*17.7*	*25.3*
Doublers	49	61	110
Percentage	*0.6*	*0.7*	*0.6*
Weavers	4,169	1,105	5,275
Percentage	*48.9*	*12.9*	*30.9*
Finishers	734	597	1,331
Percentage	*8.6*	*7.0*	*7.8*
Total	7,761	3,286	11,047
Percentage	*91.1*	*38.3*	*64.6*
Multi-process firms	756	5,287	6,043
Percentage	*8.9*	*61.7*	*35.4*
Total all firms	8,517	8,574	17,091
Percentage	*100*	*100*	*100*

Source : Statistical Appendix.

(b) *The re-equipment phase*

While the scrapping schemes inevitably affected the structure of the industry, since they led to the elimination of some firms and to adjustments in the size and structure of others, the re-equipment schemes were not in any way bound to bring about structural changes. In fact the industry's structure, as well as its size, changed very considerably between 1959 and 1964—the year the re-equipment schemes were supposed to be concluded—but it is difficult to tell how far, if at all, these changes were a consequence of re-equipment. Other powerful forces affecting the industry's shape were its continuing rapid decline, mainly though not altogether the result of continuing pressure from imports, and the rapid concentration among the larger firms that began in the first half of 1964 and continued through into 1965, inspired by the man-made fibre producers. A full discussion of the strength and effects of these various influences is deferred to the next chapter. For the present, we shall be concerned with the data on the size and distribution of re-equipment grants, and the evidence yielded about the scale of re-equipment that took place during the period covered by the provisions of the Act.

The basis on which the following table has been prepared requires a word of explanation. As re-equipment was spread over several years, and as the size and structure of the industry changed very considerably during these years, a way of relating data on applications for re-equipment grants to data on employment and structure had to be devised to provide a basis for analysis. Some firms that applied for re-equipment grants went out of business before they took them up, some went out of business after re-equipping, while some—the most important group—merged or were taken over between the time they started re-equipment and the time they finally received a grant. It was therefore necessary to choose a base date immediately after the actual physical process of re-equipment was completed, in the second half of 1964. However, between July 1964, by which date firms were supposed to have finished installing their new plant, and the middle of 1965, by which time payments of grants to individual firms were settled barring a small handful of cases, the structure of the industry was further transformed by take-overs and mergers. Thus the firms that got the grants were not necessarily those that had planned and carried through re-equipment. The compromise chosen was to use employment data for October 1964 (the nearest convenient date to the completion of re-equipment schemes), classified by the grouping of firms that existed in October 1965. The data therefore overstate total employment—by about 7 per cent—but give a better picture of the distribution of the ultimate beneficiaries of the scheme than would data on the structure of the industry as it was in October 1964.

Table 4.6 shows the structure of the industry in October 1965 and, with the exception of finishing, the numbers and employment of firms that received re-equipment grants. It also shows, for each type of firm, the total expenditures eligible for grants. Full data are not yet available for the finishing sector, as this part of the scheme has taken considerably longer to wind up than the rest.

Table 4.6. *1959 Act re-equipment: structure of industry at October 1965, number of firms receiving grants and total expenditure on re-equipment, by type of firm*

Type of firm	All firms		Firms not in scheme		Firms in scheme		Total eligible[a] expenditure on re-equipment (£'000)
	Number	Employment October 1964	Number	Employment October 1964	Number	Employment October 1964	
Single-process firms							
Spinners	41	14,446	3	672	38	13,774	6,188
Doublers	45	3,670	31	1,187	14	2,483	266
Weavers	321	45,175	182	13,742	139	31,435	9,798
Finishers	128	13,042	n.a.	n.a.	n.a.	n.a.	n.a.
Multi-process firms	39	88,003	2	502	37	87,501	29,181[b]
Total all firms	574	164,338	n.a.	n.a.	n.a.	n.a.	53,525[c]

Source : Statistical Appendix.

[a] These figures relate to total expenditures eligible for grants. The actual grants paid were 25 per cent of this total.
[b] Excluding eligible expenditure in the finishing sector.
[c] Including £8,084,000 approved expenditure in the finishing sector.

A full discussion of the extent of the structural changes in the industry between 1959 and 1965 is reserved for chapter 6. But it may be noted in the present context that the firms staying outside the scheme were small, with a mean size of 74 employees.[1] The mean size of the firms in the scheme was 250 for single-process firms (again excluding finishers), and 2,360 for multi-process firms.

Thus, as might have been predicted, it was the bigger firms and particularly the multi-process firms, that undertook some re-equipment. The numbers of new machines installed were not large in relation to total machinery in place at October 1965, as table 4.7 shows.

Table 4.7. *Machinery installed under the 1959 Act as a percentage of the total machinery installed, October 1965*

Thousands	Total installed October 1965	Installed under 1959 Act	%
Spinning spindles (ring equivalent '000)	5,216	678	*12.8*
Doubling spindles	1,024	18	*1.8*
Looms	125	11	*8.8*

Source : Cotton Board and Statistical Appendix.

However, these percentages probably underestimate the modernizing effect of re-equipment under the Act, partly because it seems likely that the new machinery installed was of higher productivity than the average, and partly because these figures do not include modifications to existing spindles and looms. This is an important way of increasing machine productivity.

[1] This does not include finishing firms staying outside the scheme. The mean size of all single-process finishing firms, applicants and non-applicants, was 102. It is unlikely, therefore, that the inclusion of the non-applicants would alter the figure of 74 by much.

CHAPTER 5

SOME COMMENTS ON THE ACT

Any attempt at an evaluation of the 1959 Act has to deal with two major questions. The first is whether it was necessary at all. Given that the industry was in some sense too large, could its size have been reduced other than by government intervention? The second concerns its effectiveness and appropriateness as a measure, given that official action of some kind was required. Did it bring about the results desired, and were government funds intelligently spent?

I. THE NEED FOR GOVERNMENT INTERVENTION

To begin with, we may consider the sense in which the industry was too large. We have discussed elsewhere the meaning of the term 'capacity', and pointed to some of the uncertainties inherent in it unless it is carefully defined with reference to a particular situation. However, in the cotton industry in 1957–59 there was a large amount of surplus capacity on the lowest possible definition of capacity working, a five-day, one-shift week, as the following table shows.

Table 5.1. *Machinery in place and running, and hours running per week, annual averages, 1957–9*

	In place	Running	Running as percentage in place	Hours per week per running machine
Spinning (Million spindles, ring equivalent)				
1957	18.53	13.65	74	43.1
1958	17.49	11.48	66	41.2
1959	15.26	10.32	68	43.8
Weaving[a] (Thousand looms)				
1957	276.0	222.7	81	49.9
1958	255.4	192.0	75	49.6
1959	222.6	172.1	77	52.0

Source : Cotton Board.

[a] Looms in place in the Lancashire area only, plus looms running in the rest of U.K. There were 12,000–15,000 running looms outside the Lancashire area.

About a third of the spindles and a quarter of the looms installed were completely idle, while the running machinery was worked on average slightly less than a full five-day week of 45 hours for spinning, and rather over the standard working week for weaving. There can be no doubt, therefore, about the existence of surplus plant in the industry.[1] It was argued that this surplus plant, all of which was fully written-off, was a threat to other producers mainly because it made possible 'weak selling' in times of strong demand for cotton goods, and this tended to depress prices below the level at which producers operating modern plant and having to meet capital costs, could cover their total costs of output and accumulate funds for re-equipment. The various steps in this argument may be examined separately.

First, there is the important assumption that labour to work the marginal plant could be found. If no labour was available, the plant would have had no value except as scrap. The statement of this assumption brings us to the heart of a paradox, discussed more fully in the next chapter, that labour apparently could be found to work marginal plant on a more or less casual basis, while at the same time other firms were complaining that they could not recruit the labour they required to maintain production. Briefly, the explanation of this situation can be traced to three facts: (i) the geographical immobility of labour, which meant that it preferred casual work nearer home to regular employment farther away; (ii) the tendency of marginal spinning mills (many of them operating mule spindles) to employ elderly men, the last survivors of a dying craft; (iii) the fact that most small weaving sheds were staffed by women, many of them married and needing jobs near their homes. Clearly these three facts are interconnected; elderly workers and women tend to be less mobile than the young, and also more reluctant to accept re-training, even if other firms had been prepared to take them on, while the weaving labour force tended to be immobile for family reasons.

Second, it may be queried why, if the 'marginal' producers operating surplus plant could undercut the other producers, they did not do this all the time. It is hard to see, in other words, why they were marginal producers at all. Here the explanation seems to lie mainly in the way in which trade in cotton textiles was organized—and still is, to some extent. The essentials of the traditional system have been described in detail by Robson, in his study of the cotton industry in Britain. The key figure was the converter, who bought grey (unfinished) cloth from a weaver, had it finished—i.e. bleached, dyed or printed—usually on a commission basis, and then sold it to a wholesaler or final user. When the market was very large and highly specialized this system worked efficiently. Converters became specialists in certain overseas markets,

---

[1] In a memorandum to the Estimates Committee, the President of the British Spinners' and Doublers' Association referred to a figure of 93 per cent as the optimum rate of activity (House of Commons, *op. cit.*, page 129). Owing to frequent changes in demand for counts and qualities of yarn, 100 per cent activity is unattainable.

such as the Indian, or in certain types of product, such as shirting cloths, and built up connections with weavers who also specialized in the appropriate types of cloth. Competition among the weavers for orders was closely fought, except in boom times, with the merchants able to specify minor variations, leading to small differences in price, that enabled them to play off one weaver against another. As the market shrank, and its nature changed, the system failed to adapt itself, and by 1958 there were 1,493 firms with converting activities handling a total cloth yardage of 2,030 million square yards.

Specialization had gone mad. Robson gives details of the order books of three small weaving firms during a six-month period in the mid 1950's[1] which can be summarized as follows :

	Firm A	Firm B	Firm C
Number of orders received	333	164	425
Number of different cloth warp specifications	115	129	298
Total yardage of orders	12.3 million	6.7 million	9.3 million
Number of merchants dealt with	73	32	74

The numbers of different cloth specifications ordered were in fact rather higher than the figures given, which refer to warp specifications only. But changing a warp is a major technical constraint on efficiency, whereas changing a weft raises little difficulty, since new supplies of weft are constantly being fed to the loom anyway. It may be noted that the weavers themselves approached the problem of buying yarn in much the same way: firm A in this sample bought yarn of identical specification from seven different spinners, presumably in order to take advantage of minor variations in price. In commenting on this example, Robson writes, 'It is generally agreed that the unnecessary variety of cloths required from manufacturers is partly due to the activities of merchants, since the minor changes in price which can be achieved by minor changes in specification tend to make such activities profitable: on the other hand the flexibility of the industry equally assists in this'.[2]

Of the 1,493 firms with converting activities that were operating in 1958, 1,155 or 77 per cent were independent, without any formal links with weavers. But these firms only handled 45 per cent of the total cloth delivered—an average of 580,000 yards per firm. However, it was this large number of firms confronting a fairly large number of weavers— 240 out of 499—dealing in this relatively small percentage of cloth, that created the 'weak selling' problem. Robson quotes another example from a firm's order book, showing 54 orders placed by 20 different merchants for 30 different specifications of cloth, of which he says 'it is doubtful if

[1] R. Robson, *The Cotton Industry in Britain*, (Macmillan, 1957), p. 94.
[2] *ibid.*, p. 95.

the consumer could distinguish more than three different qualities in this range'.[1] The main point about this too-perfect market situation is not so much that the bigger producers were undercut to the point at which they could no longer cover their costs, but that this large group of small firms competing actively for small orders had a generally depressive effect on the price level that made it very difficult for the bigger firms to get and hold prices at a level that left them any surplus for re-investment. But the small firms could only continue to exist, it seems worth repeating, for as long as they could obtain some sort of a labour force.

Unfortunately there are no data that would permit an analysis of the costs of production with different types of plant. However various calculations that have been attempted suggest that the total costs of production for an old-fashioned weaving mill using Lancashire looms at a ratio of 4 looms per weaver are broadly comparable with the costs of production using automatic looms on two shifts with a ratio of 10–12 looms per weaver. The difference is, as one informant put it, that 'all their [the old fashioned weavers'] costs are variable, while all mine are fixed'. The weaver using modern machinery has to meet not only fixed capital costs, but also fixed labour costs, if he is to retain a skilled labour force.

The existence of surplus machine capacity in 1959 is thus well established, as is the ill-adapted production and marketing structure of the industry. But it does not follow that government intervention was necessary to bring about desirable changes, nor that if legislation of some kind was needed, the approach used was the best.

Although as we have seen earlier in this chapter the 1959 Act was largely the result of pressure from the industry, opinion in it was by no means unanimous about the need for government assistance. The main argument against financial encouragement to scrap was that mills were closing all the time anyway, and that 'closures by competition . . . would if continued have reduced the industry to its present size without external intervention or stimulus'.[2] This might have been the case. However as figure 5.1 shows, the Act did accelerate the decline in the industry's size, measured by equipment installed, and the decline was resumed at something near the 1950's rate from 1960–61 onwards. And while it is true that much of the equipment scrapped under the Act was completely idle and never likely to be used again anyway (see the previous chapter), it is also a fact that most of it could have been brought back into use, and thus constituted a potential if not an actual addition to the industry's

---

[1] *ibid.* p. 92.
[2] Allan Ormerod, 'The Prospects of the British Cotton Industry', *Yorkshire Bulletin of Economic and Social Research*, vol. 15, no. 1, May 1963, p. 9.

Figure 5.1   Capacity and capacity utilization in spinning and weaving, 1951–66.

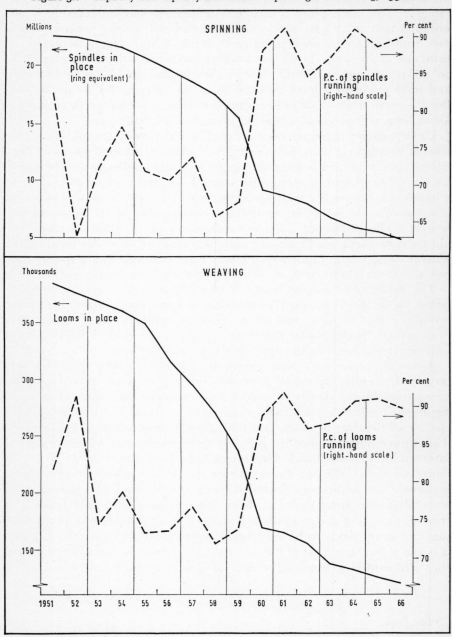

Source : Cotton Board.

capacity. The rate of scrapping might have speeded up without any extra financial inducement, and brought the industry down to its present size as quickly, but it is hard to find any specific reasons for supposing that it would.

Indeed, as has already been described, the principal ground on which those in favour of government action based their case was precisely that some special stimulus was needed to accelerate contraction. As one industry witness to the Estimates Committee hearings in 1961–2 put it, 'The process of scrapping old machinery would, in any case, have continued by natural processes but this had been found to take so long that a surgical operation was needed to remove the dead wood more quickly and put the industry into a viable position'.[1] Or, in the words of the then Chairman of the Cotton Board, 'We never reckoned that [the 1959 Act] would be the end of the process; we always reckoned that what the Government was trying to do was to provide a catalyst for getting something moving in the industry'.[2]

The Act does seem to have been quite an effective catalyst in initiating changes, although it did not have much success in bringing about the sort of structural reorganization that was required. Such, at any rate, was the view of most of those who gave evidence to the Estimates Committee. The reactions of one witness who was originally opposed to the Act make the point:

'Despite my objections I now take the view that the elimination of redundancy has been worth while. It has cleared away a mass of old plant and machinery at less cost to the community than further years of attrition. It has given a chance to progressive firms who were carrying a heavy burden of surplus capacity. It has rid the industry of a good deal of the incubus of old-fashioned management thought. It has led to an acceleration of the use of buildings for other purposes— it has accelerated the pace of diversification in Lancashire and led to a healthier economy and a better spirit'.[3]

Among these benefits claimed for the Act, the last—that it accelerated industrial diversification in Lancashire—is particularly interesting. We shall return to this point in the Appendix.

2. THE EFFECTIVENESS OF THE ACT

The industry itself objected to the form that government assistance took on two main grounds. The first was that the government's proposals were

---

[1] *House of Commons, Fourth Report from the Estimates Committee, Session 1961–62,* (1962), Memorandum by Sir Cuthbert Clegg, p. 111.

[2] *ibid.* question 209, p. 52.

[3] *ibid.,* pages 70–71, Memorandum submitted by Mr C. E. (now Sir Cyril) Harrison, then Vice-Chairman of English Sewing Cotton Co. Ltd.

not based on any serious analysis of the problem, and the second, that they penalized the more efficient units.

The charge that the government failed to analyze the situation is, as we have already shown, unanswerable. As Mr. Harrison pointed out in his memorandum to the Estimates Committee,[1] no attempt was made to find out why the pace of re-equipment was so slow, and there was no enquiry as to why inefficient mills were not driven out of business by the better equipped mills. These two points are closely related: if the better equipped mills had been able to secure a significant competitive advantage under the conditions then prevailing they would have driven out the inefficient fast, and the competitive advantage to be gained from re-equipment would have encouraged a higher rate of re-equipment. But in fact it seemed that there was little or no competitive advantage to be derived from re-equipment, given the general levels of manning and management and the market situation.

The government's failure to ask these important questions probably encouraged its optimistic delusions about the possible success of the Act. If it had asked itself these questions, and obtained the sort of answers about the technical, structural and labour problems of the industry that have been discussed in chapter 2 and elsewhere, it could hardly have sustained the hope that the measures contained in the Act were sufficient in themselves to create a healthy and competitive industry. In particular, it might have made more modest assumptions about the likely volume of re-equipment.

The second of the industry's objections, that the Act penalized the more efficient units, raises an important principle of equity. This objection centres on the burden imposed by way of levies on the efficient firms staying in the industry. 'Those who had developed and were completely equipped with ring spindles, automatic looms and finishing machinery had little to register for scrapping, they had to make large contributions to scrapping mule spindles and non-automatic looms in horizontal units, and further contributions to compensate the labour which less-efficient firms had displaced from the mass of equipment they were being paid to scrap. . . It would be hard to conceive a scheme more debilitating to the progressive, technically-sound and fully-integrated unit.'[2]

Earlier rationalization schemes, such as the 1936–9 scheme for the spinning sector, were financed by means of levies, a method that has been generally accepted as desirable and equitable. The firms staying in an industry, the argument runs, will benefit from the removal of their competitors, so it is only fair that they should contribute something towards

[1] *ibid.*
[2] Ormerod, *op. cit.* p. 9.

the costs of removal. From this point of view the government's willingness to pay two-thirds of the total was an unprecedented departure from principle, as has already been pointed out. However the question at issue is whether it was sensible to impose any part of the costs of scrapping on the firms remaining in the industry, given its prevailing weakness, with few firms making any profit in 1958–59.

In all, the industry has had to raise about £10 million for levy payments, approximately £6 million for payments in respect of machinery scrapped, including administrative costs, and about £4 million for payments to redundant labour. These levies have been collected over a period of five or seven years. It is hard to assess their burden on individual firms, but various calculations to which the author has had access suggest that it varied from under 1 per cent of total production costs to as much as 3 or 4 per cent, and even the lower figure is substantial for a firm earning little or no profit. But whatever the burden, there is a contradiction between imposing any levy on firms staying in the industry to compensate those going out, while at the same time accepting the argument that one of the basic problems of the industry was to achieve a level of profit adequate to finance re-equipment.

In tackling the question whether the Act was an effective instrument of industrial change, the difficulty is to determine just exactly what it was intended to do. The government accepted the industry's argument that help from public funds was justified to bring about a reorganized and re-equipped industry. But it did not attempt, for reasons that have been discussed, to determine an appropriate structure for the industry and then devise measures to create this structure. However, we may assume (i) that it hoped to eliminate a large proportion of the 'weak operating units barely able to pay their way',[1] primarily small weaving firms, and (ii) to encourage large scale re-equipment, to the value of £80–£100 million. How successful was the Act in achieving these two objectives?

As regards the first, we have already seen that only 23 per cent of weaving firms with 500 or fewer employees scrapped their plant at 'premium' rates and left the industry altogether. Six years later, in 1965, there were still more than 250 such firms left in the industry, over 50 per cent of the 1959 total, with a mean employment size of 130. Furthermore, the shift towards a more vertically-organized structure has been small, the proportion of total employment accounted for by multi-process firms increasing by only 7.7 per cent, from 45.9 per cent to 53.6 per cent, between 1959 and 1965.[2] It seems probable, however, that the extent of true vertical organization in the industry has increased more rapidly than these figures indicate.

[1] White Paper (Cmnd. 744), paragraph 10.
[2] See tables 4.1 and 4.6.

The Act was thus not very successful in eliminating the small weak firms, though it did accelerate the rate of contraction, if not of amalgamation and reorganization.[1] Could other, potentially more successful, measures have been devised? Higher prices for scrapped machinery might have helped, but would have been open to the objection that they imposed an additional levy burden on firms staying in the industry, unless the government had been prepared to pay a larger proportion of scrapping costs. But whether higher prices would have persuaded many more firms to leave the industry seems doubtful, as the main barrier to movement has been and still is the lack of 'mobile' management skills. For the owners of most small firms the choice lay between retirement and continuing in the same business, however small its return.

Any scheme other than one offering a fixed rate of compensation per machine or other suitable unit of capacity, payable automatically to all qualified applicants, would have required some prior conception of the shape of industry that it was intended to create. And for a true reorganization scheme to be carried through on a voluntary basis, the structure worked out would have had to be acceptable to the industry as a whole. But as any major reconstruction of the industry would have required the closing down or absorption of a very large number of firms, and not only the small ones, it is hard to see how it could have been made acceptable, and how, in short, it could have been effected.

The industry's own estimates of probable costs of re-equipment, published in the White Paper, were between £80 million and £95 million: £40 million for spinning, £8 million for doubling and £30–£45 million for weaving.[2] The finishing sectors did not anticipate that there would be much spent on re-equipment, holding the view that their problem was essentially one of contraction and reorganization of existing capacity.[3] Total eligible re-equipment expenditures under the Act in fact amounted to £53.5 million: £25.3 million for spinning, £1 million for doubling, £19.1 million for weaving and £8.1 million for finishing. Further unknown amounts have been spent on related but ineligible capital projects.

The low rate of re-equipment, in relation to the original estimates, has been mainly attributed by people within the industry to uncertainty about the import position and therefore about the size of market available to domestic producers. This point was put most forcefully in a memorandum submitted to the Estimates Committee by officials of the British

---

[1] It is hard to assess to what extent, if at all, the Act was a factor in the major reorganization of 1964–5. This question is discussed in the next chapter.

[2] Cmnd 744, paragraph 14.

[3] *ibid.* paragraph 15.

Spinners' and Doublers' Association. 'It was made clear [to the government] by the industry's representatives, however, time and again, that any scheme of government assistance and any efforts by the industry itself would be rendered useless if low-priced imports, from whatever source, were not strictly limited; if they were allowed to increase indefinitely, whether suddenly or gradually, it would not be practicable for the industry to proceed with modernization and there was a serious danger that money spent on modernization would be thrown away'.[1] In discussion, these same officials made it clear that in their view money spent on re-equipment was money wasted, in the absence of strict controls on imports.[2]

There can be little doubt that this lack of confidence in the government's intentions, and the industry's failure to obtain increased protection, was the main reason why much less was spent on re-equipment than had been anticipated. But the money not spent may well have been money not wasted, though not quite in the sense that industry's representatives meant it. For there is little indication, among published statements, that the need for a shift in the whole approach of management to the production and marketing of textiles had yet been grasped, and it seems unlikely that additional expenditure on re-equipment would of itself have done anything to improve matters.[3] It is worth recalling that the big firms taken over during the 1963–4 wave of mergers had most of them re-equipped substantially under the Act, but this did not make them viable.

We are thus brought back, once again, to the point that the Act had virtually no effect on the structure of the industry, and thus did little to improve its capacity to survive. Had imports been more strictly controlled, the rate of investment in 1961–4 would no doubt have been higher, but there is little reason to suppose that many firms would have become more efficient as a result, or that protection could have removed the need for rationalization.

3. THE FINANCIAL IMPLICATIONS OF THE ACT

The methodology of the 1959 Act, viewed as a measure intended to promote rationalization, can be criticized on several grounds as we have seen. Its financial provisions require separate examination, to determine their impact on the firms directly involved and the Lancashire textile industry in general.

[1] House of Commons, *op. cit.* p. 128. (Statement by the President of the B.S.D.A.).
[2] *ibid.*, paragraphs 779 *et seq.*
[3] The manager of a firm of textile consultants, giving evidence before the Estimates Committee, quoted the example of a firm that had spent £250,000 on new machinery and had then had to close down. 'One can find all sorts of reasons for that but the main reason is that they were unable to manage such a tool'. House of Commons *op. cit.*, paragraph 452.

The potential financial effects of the grants to the firms receiving them, and to the textile industry as a whole, are set out in tabular form below.

Scrapping grants

Return to firm	
Premium rate firms	Nil.
Other recipient firms	Cash grant available for investment.
Return to industry	Increased *average* efficiency (and hence profitability?) of all firms remaining in industry.

Re-equipment grants

Return to firm	Cash grant for approved investments.
Return to industry	No additional return, over and above returns to firms receiving grants.

Three points emerge from this analysis. First, the scrapping grants paid to premium rate firms had no economic effect on the firms themselves, since premium rate compensation was only payable to firms undertaking to leave the industry, and not to set themselves up again as textile manufacturers. The premium rate grants may, however, have had some effect on the industry as a whole, inasmuch as they led to the elimination of marginal firms and so raised average efficiency and profitability. Second, the scrapping grants paid to standard and discount rate firms augmented the cash flow of these firms. The grants could be used for investment in new plant and equipment, and were in fact less limited in their application than the re-equipment grants proper, which were only given for approved types of investment. Inasmuch as the equipment scrapped was fully written-off and rates of payment exceeded the scrap value, this additional cash flow was a pure windfall. Third, the re-equipment grants, unlike the scrapping grants, had no effect on the industry as a whole—i.e. including the firms outside the scheme—beyond their effects on recipient firms.

The grants were paid to firms as lump sums in cash. But over time, their value was reduced by two factors: first, the levies payable in respect of the scrapping schemes, and for compensation for displaced employees ; and second, the reduction in tax allowances available on investments made under the Act, as for Inland Revenue purposes the value of plant and equipment installed was computed net of the 25 per cent grant for eligible items.

Levy payments were made over a period of 5–7 years (differing in the various sectors of the industry). Of the total of £10 million collected in levies, the £4 million paid over for employees' compensation schemes plus the element of the scrapping levies that went to 'premium rate' firms—about £2.5 million—was lost to the industry. The other £3.5 million of the scrapping levies was redistributed among firms: some paid out, in total, less than they had already received in grants, while those that scrapped little or no equipment were net losers.

The netting-out of the grant element in assessing the value of investments for tax allowance purposes in effect reduced the value of re-equipment grants by the total of tax allowances foregone. This depended on the actual rate of tax payable and the assumptions made about the rate of depreciation, and cannot be calculated for the industry as a whole, or for individual firms without access to their financial records.

The costs to the industry of implementing the 1959 Act cannot therefore be fully assessed. Had the scrapping grants been 100 per cent government financed, the 'loss' of £2.5 million and the redistribution of a further £3.5 million among firms would not have occurred: had special unemployment assistance for displaced workers been made available from public funds, a loss of a further £4 million would have been averted. And in addition there was a loss of an unknown amount in tax allowances foregone.

It has already been suggested that there was some conflict between the government's policy of compelling the industry to meet part of the cost of reorganization and the major point in the government's own analysis of the situation that low profit levels were making it impossible for firms to finance re-equipment. If the government had fully accepted its own analysis, it should have been prepared to pay 100 per cent scrapping grants, possibly at lower rates, thereby not increasing the cost by the full amount of the industry's contribution.

Where re-equipment was concerned, the technique of straight cash grants may not have been the most effective in terms of the result desired. While there are arguments in favour of cash grants rather than tax allowances for new investment projects and new enterprises, where the new investment is replacing old plant the loss of tax allowances implicit in cash grants netted-out by the tax authorities must tend to penalize the firms making sufficient profits to enable them to claim their allowances in full. Re-equipment under the 1959 Act was basically of this replacement kind, and the prime need was to give some extra incentive to the most efficient firms in the industry.

The choice of straight grants, rather than some additional tax incentive working through depreciation allowances, implies the underlying supposition that what was needed was simply more investment, or a higher rate of investment. But as we have seen the problem was considerably more complicated than this: given the changing pattern of demand for the industry's products, and the structural framework existing at the time of the Act, large scale new investment was, for many firms, as likely to lead to insolvency as to more efficient production and higher profits. Had special incentives been given in the form of tax allowances, operative for a number of years, as would have been feasible under the system of investment incentives applied at the time, the total sum forgone by the revenue authorities might well have been larger than the £11.3 million paid out in re-equipment grants. But it would have been more rationally distributed, and the inevitable, and generally desirable, structural evolution now going on might have begun rather sooner.

CHAPTER 6

THE LANCASHIRE TEXTILE INDUSTRY SINCE 1959

In retrospect it seems as if the years 1958–64 marked a turning-point in the history of the Lancashire textile industry. The changes which have taken place in patterns of fibre consumption and fabric production and in corporate structure—all discussed later on in this chapter—amount to a major revision of its definition and limits. The changes themselves, and their effects, are much more fundamental than anything envisaged at the time of the 1959 Act, which was essentially aimed at raising the efficiency of the industry as it then existed, rather than transforming its very nature.[1]

The Act itself was perhaps more significant as a product of pressures for change than as an initiator of change (see the previous two chapters). In the mid-1950's, recognition by the industry of the necessity for change, as the only alternative to rapid decay and ultimate disappearance, had expressed itself more as a state of general unease than in the form of specific analysis and suggestions. Gradually three major issues emerged: the problem of the rapidly increasing flow of imports, the twin problems of the shortage of labour and stagnant levels of labour productivity, and the barriers to more efficient operation set up by the prevailing corporate and market structure. Only the first of these was new, in that imports had not seemed a problem at any previous period in the industry's history, although its decline in the 1920's and 1930's was directly associated with the loss of export markets, partly because of declining competitiveness.[2] In the previous chapters we have examined the effects of the Act on the structure of the industry: in the present chapter we shall look at recent developments on the import side, in the labour position and in productivity, before going on to consider the big changes in corporate structure and organization that are only rather remotely linked with the Act.

---

[1] The present (1967) crisis will perhaps be regarded, when it can be seen in perspective, as the collapse of much of the old Lancashire industry, complicated by the fact that the multi-fibre multi-product firms have large investments in the traditional sectors. This fact tends to obscure the fundamental changes in organization and approach that have already taken place and are still going on.

[2] Partly, also, because a number of under-developed countries started on the path to industrialization by establishing domestic textile industries—often inefficient and highly protected to begin with—and partly also because Britain's position as the world's major exporter of cotton textiles was bound to be challenged sooner or later.

I. IMPORTS[1]

The view that imports have been and still are the sole cause of the industry's difficulties, and that all would be well if they were sufficiently stringently controlled, is widely held. It is to be hoped that the analysis in the foregoing chapters of labour and structural problems of Lancashire textiles, and the slow rate of technological advance until very recently, is sufficient to demonstrate that this view is a gross over-simplification. But imports have expanded rapidly, and have created additional difficulties for an industry in the throes of decline and change. It is important, therefore, to try to evaluate their effects.

Since 1959, imports of pure cotton cloth from most of the less-developed countries have been subject to quantitative restrictions, and non-Commonwealth producers have to surmount a tariff barrier also. Imports from all other sources are unrestricted, and imports from the other member countries of the European Free Trade Area are now, since 1 January 1967, also free of tariffs.

The balance of trade in cotton and man-made fibre cloth is shown in table 6.1. In the pure cotton sector, imports have fluctuated widely, varying, in the period under review, from 537 million square yards in 1959 to 767 million square yards in 1964. In 1966, the level fell again to 587 million square yards. Exports of pure cotton piece goods, by contrast, have fallen continuously, by rather over 50 per cent between 1959 and 1966. Trade in man-made fibre cloth is of much less importance, and its balance has fluctuated around zero, with some tendency for imports to exceed exports.[2]

It is difficult to be sure of the precise effects of the restrictions, as special supplementary and carry-over provisions have meant that in most years the permitted level of imports has varied for each of the main countries concerned. In addition, the inclusion of increasing numbers of countries within the system has meant that the ratio of restricted to unrestricted imports has altered from year to year.[3] However, it is clear that the cyclical behaviour of imports cannot be attributed to restrictions, except in as far as they may damp down the peak of an import boom. During the two cycles since 1959, total import quotas have not been filled for at least half of the time, although individual categories of goods have

[1] For a fuller analysis of the import question, see the author's article 'Should the Cotton Industry be Protected?' *District Bank Review*, June 1966.

[2] The sharp fall in exports in 1966 is almost entirely accounted for by a drop of 17.3 million square yards in deliveries to the Soviet Union, the most important export market in 1963–65. British and other foreign companies have of course been supplying fibre and textile plants to the U.S.S.R. during the past few years.

[3] For details, see the article cited in footnote[1] above, pp. 48-51.

Table 6.1. *The balance of U.K. trade in cotton and man-made fibre cloth, 1959–66*

	1959	1960	1961	1962	1963	1964	1965	1966
							million square yards	
Imports								
Cotton Cloth	537	728	731	575	636	767	588	587
Man-made fibre and mixture cloth	38	58	70	66	63	93	88	93
Total	575	786	801	641	699	860	676	680
Cloth equivalent of imports of cotton made-up articles	*61*[a]	*77*[a]	*71*[a]	*156*	*157*	*182*	*148*	*180*
Exports								
Cotton cloth	347	327	287	235	222	210	205	167
Man-made fibre and mixture cloth	64	54	49	54	80	91	95	65
Total	411	381	336	289	302	301	300	232
Balance[b]								
Cotton Cloth	−190	−401	−484	−340	−414	−557	−383	−420
Man-made fibre and mixture cloth	26	− 4	− 21	− 12	17	− 2	7	− 28
Cotton Cloth, including cloth equivalent of made-up articles	*−251*	*−478*	*−555*	*−496*	*−571*	*−739*	*−531*	*−600*

Source : Cotton Board.

Note : Several changes in classification make the figures not completely comparable.
[a] From Hong Kong, India and Pakistan only.
[b] A minus sign indicates an excess of imports over exports.

gone on arriving at the full permitted rate, a point to which we shall return later on.

Grey (unfinished) cloth accounts for the bulk of imports (an average of 77 per cent in 1961–66), and we shall consider the nature of trade in grey cloth first. It seems that the interaction between production and trade cycles in Lancashire textiles is governed by the merchant converters, who buy grey cloth from foreign or domestic manufacturers, have it 'finished' by bleaching, dyeing, printing, etc., usually on a commission basis, and then sell it to a wholesaler or final user. The merchant converter is sometimes regarded as a nearly defunct figure of the 'traditional' Lancashire industry, but any firm with substantial trade interests and, or alternatively, finishing capacity, even if it also has weaving and spinning plants, is likely to consider buying foreign cloth if insufficient domestic supplies are available to maintain the throughput of its trading and/or finishing sector. The term 'converter' is therefore used as a convenient shorthand for all firms with an interest in buying cloth for processing.

Converters may be regarded as the starting point of the domestic production cycle : it is their orders for grey cloth that determine the level of production in the weaving sector and hence the demand for yarn. Together with the merchant importers, who act purely as traders, undertaking no converting of cloth either on commission or directly, they are also the starting point of the import cycle. According to some sources within the industry, the particular disruptive effects of imports arise at least in part because of the tendency of converters to increase the orders for foreign rather than for domestic cloth at the beginning of an upswing in the cycle. The effect of this move is to keep home prices down just at the point when domestic producers might expect some improvement. Once the upturn is well established, however, orders for domestic cloth also begin to rise, and so do prices.

Unfortunately no stock figures are available for a long enough period to establish fully the behaviour of stocks in the cycle. But it seems fairly clear that an important reason for the severity of successive slumps is heavy destocking. Between the end of 1964 and the end of 1966 stocks of pure cotton cloth fell by 18 per cent. During this decline at any rate (stock figures are not available for the 1961–63 slump), the impact fell more heavily on imports, which declined by 23 per cent between 1964 and 1966, than on domestic production, which declined by only 11 per cent. It thus appears that imports, large though they are in relation to total domestic consumption, do fill some sort of marginal role.

Two other points about the nature of the grey cloth trade need to be made. The first is to re-emphasize the multiplicity of sources of demand for grey cloth imports. This demand is derived not only from the merchant converters buying the cloth for finishing on commission, but also from the producing firms that need additional grey cloth as an input for their finishing plants. Imported grey cloth accounts for about a third of the total grey cotton cloth throughput of the finishing sector of the industry.

The second point concerns the complexity of the trade itself. A number of different types and widths of cloth are produced and traded, many of them with quite specific and not readily substitutable end-uses,[1] and even when total import quotas are not filled, quotas for particular types of cloth may be, and the inflow may create difficulties for individual firms and plants that cannot readily be overcome by switching production into other lines. This problem has led to pressure for increased 'categorisation' within the import quotas.

Trade in finished cloth, and in household textiles and made-up goods, does not interact with domestic production as does trade in grey cloth. It is not, therefore, of such significance in relation to the structure of the industry, except in as far as specialization along particular lines affects the sector of the domestic industry engaged in the production of similar lines, although the general level of imports, and their ratio to total domestic textile consumption, does of course affect the general level of output of the home industry.

[1] The analysis of imports published by the Cotton Board in its *Quarterly Statistical Review* includes a dozen different types of grey cotton cloth, some of them in different widths and weights per square yard. Among them are such obviously non-substitutable types as drills, canvas, terry towelling, gauze and corduroys.

2. LABOUR

The way in which a shortage of labour emerged as a factor limiting output at various points in the post-war history of the industry has been discussed elsewhere.[1] Up to the late 1950's most firms in the industry seem to have regarded labour as an input that could be varied with changes in the level of demand, as indeed for many firms it was. With this view of labour went a lack of interest in selling as opposed to production that is perhaps explicable in terms of the inability of the numerous small producers to control or influence markets, but which helped to create general misunderstandings about the true nature of the industry's problems. Alister Sutherland, discussing the case of the Yarn Spinners Agreement in the Restrictive Practices Court, comments on 'the odd treatment of a labour shortage as determined by something quite other than wage rates and working conditions' by industry witnesses, and quotes the President of the Yarn Spinners' Association as saying ' There would be no excess capacity if it were not for labour problems'.[2]

In an interesting discussion of the policy of the cotton trade unions during the 1950's, H. A. Turner describes the labour position in some detail, in connection with the unions' policies of accepting a lag in wage rates below national industrial wages, and short-time working when trade was bad. He writes :—

'Short time working had three effects. First that it permitted unmodernized firms to hang on to labour which—because in such firms labour forms a large proportion of costs—it would have put them out of business to employ full-time. It thus also limited the ability of modernized firms which had been prevented by labour shortage from exploiting new equipment fully (for instance, via shift working) before the recession, to take advantage of the latter to appropriate the unmodernized mills' labour surplus by offering it employment. Secondly, however, repeated short-time working involved reduced earnings and insecurity that drove the more mobile operatives to seek other work . . . Yet it became a commonplace that in each brief recovery since 1952 (or even during the recessions themselves) some mills were unable to put their remaining employees on full-time because of a lack of workers in some key processes.'[3]

He even goes on to argue that had the unions adopted a rather different kind of policy, a combination of acceptance of the need for greater

---

[1] See chapter 3.
[2] A. Sutherland, 'The Restrictive Practices Court and Cotton Spinning', *Journal of Industrial Economics*, October 1959, p. 74.
[3] H. A. Turner, *Trade Union Growth, Structure and Policy, op. cit.*, pp. 339-40.

mobility of occupation within the industry in return for higher wages guaranteed at a level that would make part-time working completely uneconomic, they might not only have mitigated the consequences of decline but even have done something to forestall it (p. 344). Short-term and strictly sectional views were not confined to management.

The labour shortage has not lessened during the 1960's. Indeed the underlying position is probably getting worse, as the results of the loss of some of the most productive members of the labour force during the previous decade became apparent, and as the efforts of many of the old textile towns to diversify provide other, attractive, types of employment. When the author visited a number of firms in Lancashire in the winter of 1964–65 the most frequently cited reason for not expanding output, in a period of strong demand, was inability to recruit labour.

3. PRODUCTIVITY

The changing patterns of cotton and man-made fibre yarn and cloth production since 1961 are shown in figure 6.1. For cotton yarn and cloth, the picture is one of cyclical fluctuations imposed on a declining trend. In the man-made fibres sector, yarn production declined somewhat during the early 1950's but now seems to be fluctuating about a fairly constant level, with increasing output of spun synthetic yarns compensating for further falls in spun rayon. Man-made fibre cloth production (which includes cloths woven from continuous filament yarns) has also shown no strong trend up or down since the mid-1950's.

Estimates of changes in output per man-hour since 1951 are shown graphically in figure 6.2. The indices have been derived using Cotton Board data on output, but for employment Ministry of Labour data have been used as they can be related directly to the Ministry's half-yearly data on hours worked. The results should therefore be treated with some caution, but the general trends indicated are confirmed by confidential calculations prepared by individual firms which the author has been shown. No adjustment has been made for variations in qualities and types of product, in the absence of any firm empirical data for the industry as a whole on which such adjustments could be based. But some of them could be significant, the increasing share of man-made fibre weaving, for example, and the results presented should only be regarded as crude estimates.

Allowing for cyclical fluctuations the trend in weaving has been steadier than the trend in spinning, although productivity in spinning has increased more rapidly since 1963. In both sectors, there was a marked increase in 1959–1960, the period of the 1959 Act scrapping schemes, with the spinning sector recording an increase of 9 per cent in

Figure 6.1.   Cotton and man-made fibre yarn and cloth production, 1951–66, weekly averages, seasonally adjusted.

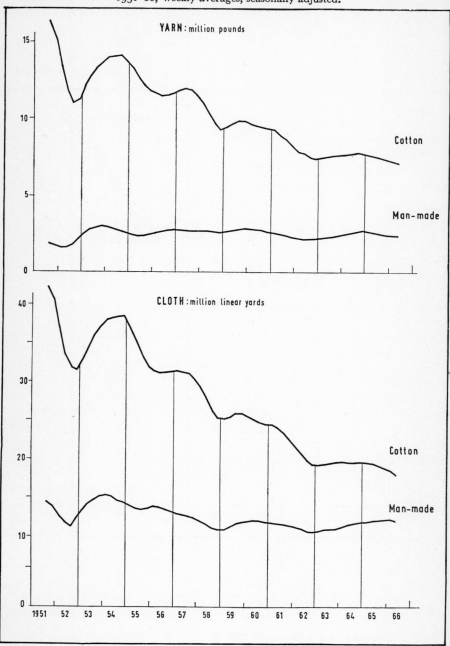

Source : Cotton Board.

Figure 6.2.   Output per man-hour in cotton and man-made fibre
spinning and weaving, 1951–66.

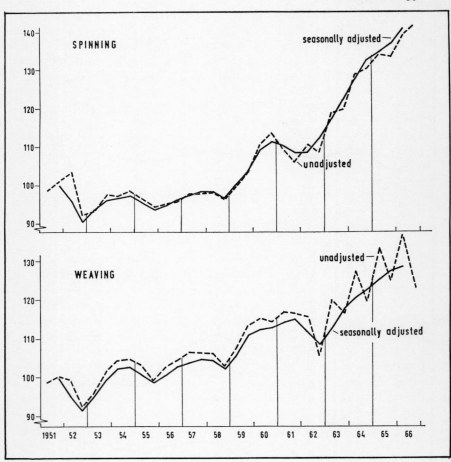

Index numbers 1951 = 100

the year 1959.I–1960.I. This pattern confirms the success of the Act in eliminating some of the least productive equipment. And from the low point of the 1961–62 downturn, productivity in both sectors rose continuously up to 1966, the improvement in spinning averaging 8 per cent annually in 1962–64, and 5 per cent annually in 1964–66.

The unadjusted figures for both spinning and weaving show an annual variation, with productivity rising faster in the second half of each year than in the first, in which indeed it quite often seems to have declined. This is particularly marked in weaving during the 1960's. The most obvious explanation for it is that there is some under-employment in the early part of the year (the main production season for next summer's trade is the autumn and winter), and probably some labour hoarding.

Under-employment, short-time working and labour hoarding are also probably the main reasons for the cyclical fluctuations in productivity which have occurred in both spinning and weaving.

There has also been an increase in the productivity of capital, measured in terms of output per machine hour. Output per ring equivalent spindle increased by 30 per cent between the beginning of 1959 and the middle of 1966, following a rise of only 2 per cent in 1951–59, and this estimate probably understates the rise in more recent years, as the ratio for converting mule to ring spindles gives too much weight to the former. The convention is to take one ring spindle as the equivalent, in productive terms, of 1.5 mule spindles. But as obtainable rates of output per ring spindle, using modern equipment, have at least doubled in the last few years, it seems rather out of date. While the point is unimportant in relation to 1965–6 figures, since mule spindles now form such a small proportion of the whole, it may possibly lead to an over-estimate of spindle hours, and thus to an under-estimate of output per spindle, in 1959–63, when the number of mule spindles was decreasing rapidly and the number of modern ring spindles was increasing slowly.

A similar qualification applies to estimates of output per loom hour, the potential rate of output of a modern automatic loom being perhaps 3 or 4 times that of a Lancashire loom. In the official Cotton Board data, however, no attempt is made to reduce the different types of looms to a common unit, and there is the added difficulty that there are no series of figures for looms with automatic attachments, but only for fully automatic looms. If data for loom hours were expressed in terms of 'automatic' loom hours the total number of hours worked would be lower than as shown in the existing data, as each non-automatic loom-hour would only count as 0.50 or 0.25 of an automatic loom-hour. Rates of output per hour per loom would thus be higher than calculated from the existing data, but would appear to have risen less between 1951, when automatics are estimated to have been 10 per cent of the total, and 1965, when they were 27 per cent.   Estimates of output per hour calculated from the available figures show a rise of 10 per cent between 1951 and 1959, and a rise of 14 per cent between 1959 and mid-1965.

These rates of increase for the industry as a whole are very low in relation to the potential rates of output per hour obtainable from modern equipment as compared with conventional equipment of the 1950's.[1] This would be the case for weaving even if the figures were adjusted to take reasonable account of the difference in productive capacity between automatic and Lancashire looms.   Such increases in output per machine per hour as have been achieved can be attributed partly to the elimination of the most inefficient equipment, partly to the installation of a certain amount of new machinery (though this has been modest in relation to the total, see chapter 4, p. 65), partly to the use of existing machinery at higher speeds, particularly in spinning, and partly, it seems probable, to the improved organization of production in individual mills.[2]

4. THE CHANGING PATTERN OF FIBRE CONSUMPTION

During the 1960's the full significance of the shift from cotton to man-made fibres,[3] and the accompanying growth in knitted as opposed to woven fabrics, has become plain.   Table 6.2 shows what has been happening.

Table 6.2.   *Cotton and man-made fibre yarn consumption in weaving and knitting, 1959–66*

	1959	1960	1961	1962	1963	1964	1960=100 1965	1966
Weaving								
Cotton	100	100	93	81	80	80	77	70
Man-made fibres[a]	94	100	94	89	95	104	106	100
Total	98	100	94	84	85	88	87	81
Knitting[b]								
Cotton	107	100	86	87	106	104	97	94
Man-made fibres[a]	81	100	110	124	171	211	234	251
Total	94	100	98	111	138	157	166	172
Total yarn consumption, weaving and knitting	97	100	94	87	92	97	97	93

Source : Cotton Board.

[a] Continuous filament and spun, and including mixtures.
[b] Years run from 1 February to 31 January. 1966 figures are estimated from data for first three quarters.

[1] Ormerod, *Yorkshire Bulletin, op. cit.* suggests a trebling of weaving speeds, using Sulzer looms, and a doubling of spinning speeds.
[2] See Cummins, *Viyella International, op. cit.*
[3] Now formally recognised in the creation of the Textile Council in place of the old Cotton Board.

The most startling feature is the rapid growth of consumption of man-made fibres by the knitting industry. It has increased by over two and a half times since 1960, with synthetic yarns,[1] both continuous filament and spun, showing by far the most rapid rate of growth. Weaving is still much more important in absolute terms, the volume of yarn consumed weekly in 1965 averaging 11.25 million lbs. for weaving compared with 3.32 million lbs. for knitting.

Warp and circular knitted cloths have made substantial inroads into a number of markets formerly supplied by the Lancashire weaving industry. Knitted underwear and knitted shirts are perhaps the most familiar of these, but there has been rapid growth in the production of outerwear fabrics—for dresses, shirts, suits and so on—and knitted sheets and household fabrics are also of significance. In the weaving sector, the only important increases in output have been recorded in continuous filament man-made fibre cloths (both rayon and synthetic). Tyre cord and mixture fabrics have just about held their own, in absolute terms, but the output of virtually all types of cotton cloth has declined by between 20 and 30 per cent.

Without making a detailed analysis of the nature of hosiery and knitted cloth output, for which data are not available over a sufficient period of time, it is impossible to be sure how far knitting has grown at the expense of woven cotton and man-made fibre textiles, in terms of competing end-products, and how far at the expense of other sectors of the textile industry, or to what extent it has developed new products and new markets for knitted textiles. The data available for 1966 only[2] suggest strongly that much of the growth in warp knitting must have been at the expense of woven textiles: 95 per cent of cloth output was for apparel uses, including such items as underwear, shirts, dresses, blouses and linings, and of the remaining 5 per cent, 4 per cent was for sheets and curtain nets. The hosiery sector is not so directly competitive, but the development of knitted clothing (soft sports shirts, etc.), must also have had some adverse effect on the demand for woven cloths.

In general, the importance of both warp and circular knitting in the production of textiles for purposes formerly met by woven fabrics is now well established, and on these grounds alone it is impossible, any longer, to understand or analyse the problems of the 'Lancashire woven' sector in isolation. It has been one of the factors leading to a re-organization of the structure of the textile industry, to which we may now turn.

---

[1] See chapter 2 for a description of the main types of man-made fibre yarns.
[2] Published for the first time in the Summer 1967 issue of the Textile Council's *Quarterly Statistical Review*.

5. CHANGES IN STRUCTURE

In the previous chapter it was shown how the 1959 Act reduced the number of firms in the industry by about 21 per cent, through the offer of 'Premium Rate' compensation for equipment scrapped to firms leaving the textile industry altogether. Table 6.3 summarizes these changes, together with the changes between 1959 and 1965. During

Table 6.3. *Changes in numbers of firms in the Lancashire textile industry,*
1959–65

Type of firm	April 1959	Less Premium Rate firms	End 1959	Change, end 1959–1965	October 1965
Single-process firms					
Spinners	86	— 36	50	— 9	41
Waste spinners	23	—	23	— 4	19[a]
Doublers	75	— 7	68	— 23	45
Weavers	567	—123	444	—122	322
Finishers	177	— 30	147	— 19	128
Total	928	—196	732	—177	555
Multi-process firms	58	— 7	51	— 12	39
Total, all firms	986	—203	783	—189	594

Source : Statistical Appendix

[a] Figure supplied by Cotton Board Statistics Department.

this period there was considerable further contraction in both the single-process and the multi-process groups of firms. Among the single-process firms it was sharpest, in percentage terms, in doubling and weaving firms, which were reduced by 34 and 27 per cent respectively, while among the much smaller group of multi-process firms 24 per cent were eliminated. However, a distinction must be made between the nature of the contraction in the two groups. While most firms in the former group that disappeared between the end of 1959 and 1965 were probably businesses leaving the industry altogether, many of the disappearances in the latter were the result of take-overs and mergers.

Table 6.4 analyses the changes between 1959 (before the Act) and 1965 in more detail, and also shows how the numbers employed, and their distribution, changed.

The total number of firms in the industry, excluding waste-spinning firms, fell by 344 (40 per cent) between 1959 and 1965. Taken as a whole, the single-process group of firms contracted only slightly faster than the multi-process group, and there were still 514 single-process firms with 500 or fewer employees left in the industry in October 1965, of which 314 were weavers. Among multi-process firms, the most striking contraction, in terms of numbers, is in the large firms, those with 2,000 or

Table 6.4.　*Number of firms and employment, by type and size of firm, April 1959 and October 1965*

Type of firms	Size range	0–500	501–1000	1001–2000	2001 and over	All sizes	Employment[a] (thousands)	% Total Employment
Single-process firms								
Spinners	1959	69	13	2	2	86	33.4	*13.9*
	1965	32	8	1	—	41	14.4	*8.8*
	Change	− 37	− 5	− 1	− 2	− 45		
Doublers	1959	73	2	—	—	75	5.5	*2.3*
	1965	44	—	1	—	45	3.7	*2.3*
	Change	− 29	− 2	+ 1	—	− 30		
Weavers	1959	546	17	4	—	567	71.4	*29.8*
	1965	314	6	1	1	322	45.2	*27.5*
	Change	−232	−11	− 3	+ 1	−245		
Finishers	1959	166	7	2	2	177	27.7	*11.6*
	1965	124	3	—	1	128	13.0	*7.9*
	Change	− 42	− 4	− 2	− 1	− 49		
Total, single-process firms[a]	1959	854	39	8	4	905	138.0	*57.6*
	1965	514	17	3	2	536	76.3	*46.5*
	Change	−340	−22	− 5	− 2	−369		
Multi-process firms	1959	15	18	8	17	58	101.3	*42.4*
	1965	11	11	10	7	39	88.0	*53.5*
	Change	− 4	− 7	+ 2	−10	− 19		
Total, all firms	1959	869	57	16	21	963	239.3	*100*
	1965	525	28	13	9	575	164.3	*100*
	Change	−344	−29	− 3	−12	−388		

Source : Statistical Appendix.

[a] Excluding waste spinners.

more employees, which fell from 17 to 7. The proportion of total employment in this same group of large firms rose considerably, from 30 to 38 per cent. These apparently contradictory movements are a result of a number of mergers and take-overs, discussed in the following paragraphs.

The growth of the main Lancashire textile companies between 1957/8 and 1965/6, measured in terms of net assets employed, and the effects of take-overs and mergers on their relative positions are shown in table 6.5. The selection of companies shown in this table is inevitably somewhat arbitrary. It leaves out two large specialist companies, Turner & Newall (industrial textiles) and Smith & Nephew (surgical textiles) with net assets in 1963/4 of £92 million and £19 million respectively, and it also leaves out textile companies outside the 'Lancashire' sector that have been taken over by Lancashire firms. Strictly speaking Viyella International was not originally a Lancashire firm, but as its impact on the Lancashire textile industry is so important it has been included in the list. Of the companies that are included, the two largest, Courtaulds and J. & P. Coats, Patons & Baldwins, have major interests outside Lancashire textiles. Courtaulds' total textile assets in 1965/6 were estimated by the

Table 6.5. *Major cotton and man-made fibre textile companies: ranking by net assets, 1957/8, 1960/1, 1963/4, 1965/6*

	1957/8[a]		1960/1[a]		1963/4[a]		1965/6		£ million Growth in net assets 1957/8-1965/6 (1957/8=100)
	Net assets	Ranking	Net assets	Ranking	Net assets	Ranking	Net assets	Ranking	
Courtaulds	169.24	1	207.77	1	262.38	1	308.72	1	183
J. & P. Coats, Patons & Baldwins	76.16	2	(80.0)	(2)	120.06	2	136.83	2	
Lancashire Cotton Corp.	25.51	3	26.67	5	25.52	5	Courtaulds 1964		175
Calico Printers Association	25.00	4	27.63	3	29.78	4	43.66	5	204
English Sewing Cotton	23.03	5	27.22	4	38.79	3	46.92	3	
Fine Spinners & Doublers	22.70	6	21.94	6	21.84	6	Courtaulds 1964		
Bradford Dyers Association	11.74	7	10.98	8	10.75	9	Viyella 1964		
Bleachers' Assn. (now Whitecroft Ind. Hdgs)	10.20	8	12.54	7	12.02	8	14.16[b]	7	
Combined English Mills	9.95	9	9.03	9	8.80	10	Viyella 1964		
Amalgamated Cotton Mills Trust	8.10	10	8.67	10	Viyella 1963				
Wm. Hollins & Co. (now Viyella International)	4.58	11	4.76	11	19.37	7	45.21	4	985
Horrockes, Crewdson & Co.	4.51	12	J. & N. Philips 1960						
Barlow & Jones	3.11	13	3.31	13	3.08	14	E.S.C. 1964		
D. Whitehead & Sons (Holdings)	3.01	14	4.55	12	5.53	12	8.01	8	267
Carrington & Dewhurst	2.53	15	2.93	14	6.91	11	21.14	6	835
Ashton Bros. Ltd. (Holdings)	2.41	16	2.68	15	5.15	13	7.73	9	320

Source : Board of Trade, *Company Assets and Income in 1957* (H.M.S.O. 1960), *Company Assets, Income and Finance in 1960* (H.M.S.O. 1962), *Company Assets, Income and Finance in 1963* (H.M.S.O. 1965). Figures for 1965 have been taken from company accounts, and may not be wholly comparable.

[a] For each company, net assets at the end of its financial year falling between 6 April and 5 April—for example, between 6 April 1957 and 5 April 1958.

[b] For 31 March 1965.

company to be £70 million, of which the greater part represents Lancashire textile interests. No figures are available for the proportion of the total net assets of J. & P. Coats in Lancashire textiles, where the company's main activity is the production of sewing threads of different types from cotton and man-made fibres. A further reason for not attaching too great a significance to the ranking shown is that all figures are for group assets, including overseas subsidiaries, and that some of the companies listed, notably J. & P. Coats, English Sewing Cotton, Viyella and Carrington & Dewhurst, have foreign textile manufacturing interests. For the first two of these companies manufacturing operations abroad are a substantial part of group activity.

Nevertheless, the table does show the major changes that have occurred since 1957/8, both in the number of large companies surviving in the Lancashire textile industry and in their relative importance. Of the 16 largest companies in 1957/8, only 9 were still in existence at the beginning of 1966, while of the 7 companies that had disappeared 6 had been bought by 3 of the remaining 9: 3 by Viyella, 2 by Courtaulds, and 1 by English Sewing Cotton. The seventh company to disappear, Horrockses, Crewdson & Co., was bought by J. & N. Philips and Co. in 1960. These six major take-overs are only a fraction of the total number of companies bought by the big firms. A rough estimate based on information published in company accounts and newspaper reports suggests that the main buyers—Courtaulds, English Sewing Cotton, Viyella and the Calico Printers' Association, Carrington & Dewhurst and Ashton Brothers— may have between them bought 100–150 companies since 1960. This figure includes as separate units the companies that made up the relatively loosely organized groups such as Combined English Mills and Fine Spinners and Doublers.[1] The last point is an important one: some of the major acquisitions made in 1963–4 were of holding companies rather than of integrated manufacturing businesses, and the task of rationalizing their productive facilities and integrating them with other textile activities is having to be dealt with unit by unit.

6. CONCLUSIONS

The instability that has characterized the Lancashire textile industry for the past fifty years—with a few brief periods of relative calm—still persists. It would be rash to try to predict how it will be eliminated, or

---

[1] 'At the time of the take-over by Viyella, the [C.E.M.] group was composed of 14 traditional spinning mills, each operating as a separate trading concern, loosely connected but not fully controlled by a headquarters staff. It also had eight subsidiary trading companies engaged in various allied activities, also operating as separate businesses.' (Ernest Cummins, 'Combined English Mills, A Case Study in Rationalization', in *Viyella International*, Autumn 1966). Combined English Mills, Fine Spinners & Doublers and the Lancashire Cotton Corporation were all originally formed to amalgamate numbers of smaller spinning companies.

when. Nevertheless, there are certain features of the present situation which, taken together, and they are all to a varying extent interdependent, suggest possible lines of development. Three factors that seem to the author to be of prime importance for the future are the changing nature of the industry, its inputs and outputs; the technological/economic argument on the issue of long runs and mass production versus specialization and diversification; and the evolving ownership structure. They are discussed in the following paragraphs, together with some further consideration of the import question, which is of interest in as far as it relates to them, to the second in particular.

All these matters take us considerably beyond the scope of the 1959 Act, and are only to a minor degree results of it. This, however, is a reflection on the deficiencies of that particular attempt at government sponsored rationalization, and the thinking that lay behind it, and should not be taken to imply that the problems of definition and nature, technology and economics and structure and organization are irrelevant. Indeed any further thinking on rationalization needs to start with a consideration of the factors that make it necessary, rather than going straight for a superficial effort to treat the symptoms.

(a) The changing nature of the industry, its inputs and outputs

The increasing complexity of the pattern of raw fibre use, and the growth of other forms of textile fabric manufacture as competitors in areas of consumption formerly satisfied by woven fabrics, are by now well established. The creation of a Textile Council for the Man-made Fibre, Cotton and Silk Industries in place of the old Cotton Board is an indication that officialdom has moved some way towards recognizing this change,[1] though it can be argued that acceptance will only be complete when it is acknowledged that all the different 'industries'—cotton, wool, man-made fibres, silk, jute, warp knitting, hosiery, lace, etc.—are parts of a single textile industry.

A major effort at re-definition and re-thinking of this kind could help in the analysis of sectoral problems. The sources of competition are often not confined to more efficient producers of the same product, or to 'low cost' producers in other countries, but extend to producers of some quite different product, serviceable for the same range of end-uses, that has a significant advantage in price and, or alternatively, quality. This way of looking at things raises important questions for company policy, that are taken up again in section *(d)*.

The changes taking place in the outlets for textile products are also

---

[1] In addition it has recently been reported that the textile unions have agreed to abandon the Labour Party's 1957 'Plan for Cotton' on the grounds that it no longer makes sense to deal with cotton's problems in isolation.

having an impact on the industry itself. About 50 per cent of Lancashire's fabric production goes to the clothing industry, and here it meets strong foreign competition in the market in selling to industrial consumers who regard fabric as their main raw material, and are influenced by many factors including consistency of quality and reliability of delivery as well as price when choosing suppliers. (The same is true, to a considerable extent, one step lower down the production ladder, in the finishing sector. Grey cloth is the raw material of the finishing industry, just as finished cloth is of the clothing industry.)

The clothing manufacturers, in turn, are affected by current developments in retail trading techniques. The growth of mail order houses and multiple stores selling their own branded goods (e.g. Marks and Spencer) has tended both to keep prices down, because of the aggressive buying policies they have been able to adopt, and to set standards of quality of fabric and manufacture, and reliability in delivery, that the mass of smaller retailers was never able to achieve. Mail order houses have increased their sales more than eightfold in the last fifteen years, and now may account for up to 20 per cent of total sales of household textiles, and perhaps 7–10 per cent of clothing.[1] The multiple stores' share of retail textile sales rose from 30 to 37 per cent between 1954 and 1964.

Apart from the clothing industry (50 per cent), household textiles (25 per cent), and carpets (10 per cent), the main markets for Lancashire textiles are industrial, and rather more fragmented. Non-textile substitutes are available in many of them—car upholstery, tyre cord, belting—and competition is strong. But on the other hand opportunities may exist, at present unexploited, for textile products to win a share in markets that they have not yet penetrated.

The general conclusion of this section, therefore, is that the nature of the industry is being altered mainly for technological reasons: the development of new man-made fibres and related developments in their processing. It is also being affected by the changing market situation for its products which again cannot altogether be divorced from the fibre revolution, although there are other factors at work, notably the shifting pattern of retail trade. As yet it has not adapted itself fully to these changes, which themselves are anyway by no means at an end. Indeed the crucial need at this stage is perhaps still for a more general recognition of the necessity to come to terms with the present evolving situation.

(b) Imports

The de-stabilising effect of imports seems to derive partly from the wide

---

[1] There are not many figures available, but the 1961 Census of Distribution showed mail order houses as accounting for 10.6 per cent of total retail sales of household textiles, 6.5 per cent of women's and children's clothing and 5.4 per cent of men's and boys' wear. The proportions have certainly risen since then.

variety of technically non-substitutable fabrics produced domestically and imported, and partly from the system of administration of the quotas themselves. The first of these factors is the more important. Concentration of imports on a particular weak sector of the domestic weaving industry—pile fabrics, drills, jeans and gaberdines, and sheetings (woven on extra wide looms) are among those that have been attacked at one time or another—can result in mill closures and consequent unemployment, where it is technologically difficult and expensive, if not impossible, to switch production to other types of cloth. The main problem created by the system of administration is that because of the 'carry-over' provisions incorporated in it, under which quotas unused in one year can be carried forward into the early part of the next, the delivery of imports has tended to be uneven. And for the sector of the weaving industry dependent on merchants' orders, this obviously leads to difficulties in planning output.

When, as in the first quarter of 1967, there is import concentration on a particular market (in this case sheeting) from an uncontrolled source (Portugal) facing a zero tariff (following the completion of the elimination of tariffs within E.F.T.A.), following a poor summer, and the effect of all these factors is intensified by a major recession, it is not surprising that the fall in domestic production has been sharp.[1] However, there is no reason to suppose that imports have been the most important factor at work: the squeeze and the recession have had a major impact on the industry, and by their depressive effects on the whole economy have made it more difficult for displaced labour to find other employment, and so highlighted the problems created by mill closures.

It is quite unrealistic to suppose that the volume of imports will be sharply reduced by government action. The major political problems of the United Kingdom's relationships with the developing world alone make it most unlikely. Furthermore, the domestic industry is now so reduced in size and capacity that a degree of restriction sufficient to protect the marginal producers in the most uncompetitive sectors of the trade would create major problems of supply for the market as a whole, and difficulties for the sectors of the textile and clothing industries dependent on imported cloth as a 'raw material' input.

The problem, therefore, is to what extent it is possible to integrate imports with the rest of the industry so as to reduce their unpredictability and hence their de-stabilising effects on production plans. This problem would seem to be partly economic and technological, in that the structure of costs and the technology employed are determinants of competitive positions in different sectors of the fabric market, and partly one of

---

[1] Though it may be noted that the *rate* of decline of cloth production over the past year has not so far been as rapid as in the 1951–2 recession.

finding an appropriate structure that takes full account of the great importance of marketing problems. These points are taken up in the next two sections.

(c) Economic and Technological Problems

Two basic economic problems face the industry at the present time: the need to adapt its product structure to current market conditions, and the need to control its production costs. These problems cannot be separated from each other, or from consideration of the range of productive techniques available, as the choice of technique is an important determinant of cost structure.

The problem of adaptation to market conditions is taken up in the final section. The object of this section is to emphasize the complexity of the economic and technological problems and choices that textile firms face, and to attempt some clarification of them. This complexity is most evident at the level of fabric production; in the present context this means weaving, provided that it is always borne in mind that the main alternative production technique—knitting—is appropriate and competitive for many end-uses.

The output of the spinning sector is largely determined by the level of demand for yarn in weaving and knitting, together with the yarn import situation. The main long-run factor here, apart from general market considerations, is the trend in fibre technology: in recent years the decline in spun rayon output has been just about offset by increasing output of spun synthetic, but the future level of output of spun man-made fibre yarns must be largely dependent on technological developments.

We return therefore to weaving. Here, as in spinning, the general thinking underlying the 1959 Act re-equipment grants, and much discussion since, has been that the only way to cut costs is to invest in the most up-to-date, labour-saving machinery, run it on multiple shifts in order to reduce its capital costs per unit of output, and still manage to cut labour costs per unit (despite shorter working hours, shift and night work premiums, etc.) enough to make a reduction in total costs per unit of output possible. Unfortunately, this single-minded emphasis on labour (and capital) productivity tends to obscure the point that the success of the whole approach depends on being able to sell the output at a price that will cover costs, or, to put the point in another way, that the cost reductions obtained by re-equipment must be large enough to make the product competitive in the market.

This theory also implies long runs of output, as it can easily be demonstrated that the higher the speed of the machine, the more output is lost by stopping to make changes in warp or weft, or in the construction of the cloth. But the non-homogeneous nature of output and the fact that a considerable proportion of it, at least 50 per cent, is affected by changes in fashion and taste means that the opportunities for long runs are limited. Furthermore up to the present the standard types of cloth have proved to be particularly vulnerable to competition from imports. This vulnerability arises not just from lower labour costs in competing countries, but also from lower capital costs, obtained through more intensive utilization of equipment. Taking two-shift working (4,160 hours/year) as a standard, a recent G.A.T.T. study found that in weaving, the U.K. worked on average one and a half shifts, Portugal (and most other European countries) nearly two shifts, India two and a half shifts, and Hong Kong nearly four shifts, or virtually full time all the year round.[1]

At the moment no reliable comparative cost data are available[2] that make it possible to determine whether, given the present level of labour costs, British firms installing modern weaving machinery and working a three-shift week could compete with imports. There is evidence that some firms think they can, particularly if they can obtain further reductions in capital costs by establishing plants in development areas—thus incidentally moving out of the old textile areas of Lancashire altogether, under present policies for the distribution of industry. But even given investment grants a substantial amount of capital is required to set up a completely new plant, and only a handful of companies in the industry can command the necessary financial resources and management and marketing skills.

For the rest, the problem of what to produce remains crucial. And the only possible way forward for them, apart from some specialists with strong established market links, seems to be through arrangements that will keep them more closely in touch with what the market wants. Some smaller firms have already formed direct links (not necessarily involving formal financial arrangements) with multiple stores and mail order houses. But there is perhaps scope for a more general attempt by weavers and finishers, the two groups most affected, to strengthen their position in relation to the merchants and to take a more active interest in the marketing of their own products.

(d) Structure and marketing

The arguments for changes in the textile industry's structure are based on two considerations: the economic, technical, and financial reasons for increasing the size of textile enterprises—though not necessarily of

---

[1] General Agreement on Tariffs and Trade, *A Study on Cotton Textiles* (Geneva, 1966), Statistical Appendix part II table D. The United States industry works three shifts, and the Japanese just over two.

[2] Neither the G.A.T.T. study quoted above nor the recent O.E.C.D. study, *Modern Cotton Industry* (Paris, 1965) attempted any cost comparisons, though both commented on the difficulties of doing so.

plants—and the market problem. The second now seems the more important, though most earlier rationalization attempts have been based on economic and financial reasoning rather than on an analysis of the structural and market situation.

Certainly many of the very small plants still in existence, especially in weaving and finishing, are plainly uneconomic in the longer run, in the sense that they are not able to make adequate depreciation provisions to cover the cost of re-equipment that will ultimately be necessary for survival, and would seem to have little future. On the other hand, the optimal size of a modern textile plant is not particularly large, according to various sources,[1] perhaps around 50,000 spindles and 1,000 looms (a little over 1 per cent of present—1966—U.K. running capacity), and from the strictly technical point of view there may not be much advantage to be gained from operating several optimal sized plants within the same firm, although the external economies possible in management and marketing may be considerable. It should be borne in mind that the wholesale acquisition of firms—many of them already large— by a few big companies in 1963/64 did not lead at once to increasing efficiency and profitability, but initially at least to just the opposite.

On financial grounds, as distinct from technical grounds, there are, however, stronger arguments for increased size. The capital costs of re-equipment with modern machinery are high,[2] and only larger enterprises are likely to possess or be able to command the necessary resources. Indeed it is increasingly clear that what the big companies are having to do is to scrap many of the inefficient units they bought three or four years ago and either completely re-equip existing buildings, drawing on the available displaced labour force, or put up entirely new plants, sometimes outside the traditional textile areas.

But the logic underlying all these technical and financial moves must be the logic of the market situation in which the textile industry is operating. This of course includes, besides the product market, the fibres market. When the two big man-made fibre producers transformed the corporate structure of Lancashire textiles in 1963/4 (see section 5 of this chapter), one reason advanced for their action was their need to secure outlets for their fibres, which estimates of future world capacity suggested would soon come under strong pressure. Since then most fibre prices have fallen considerably, and foreign fibre producers are beginning to invade the British market, adding to the intensity of competition (domestic fibre producers continue to be large exporters). One

[1] See, for example, Allan Ormerod, 'Integration of the Textile Industry', *The Investment Analyst*, May 1965, and O.E.C.D., *op. cit.*

[2] One estimate suggests £6,000–£7,500 per worker, for a plant employing 600 (700 including administrative staff)—i.e., a total cost of between £3.5 million and £5.0 million. (Estimate by Ormerod, quoted in O.E.C.D. *op. cit.*, page 97).

way of meeting this situation is obviously to try to maintain a technological and market lead in the development of new fibres or variants with special properties, and here the fibre producer with a large direct interest in textiles would appear to have certain advantages, both technologically and in creating markets for the finished products manufactured from the fibres. It must be observed, however, that this is not the view of most of the world's fibre producers, who have chosen to stay out of textile manufacture altogether.

In a situation where a good part of the product market is in a perpetual state of uncertainty owing to changes in taste and fashion—and in textiles this is true of much of the apparel sector (50 per cent of the whole), an increasing proportion of the household textiles sector (25 per cent), and some fraction of the industrial sector (car upholstery fabrics, for example) —any reorganization that brings producers into more direct contact with the feel of their markets is likely to help them. The recent changes in ownership structure are certainly doing just this. The approach of the new men in Lancashire is plainly a long way from the view that the market is there to take the goods that producers are best equipped to turn out, a view that prevailed long after the conditions that had made it tenable had disappeared. It is not clear why the merchants, who in the days when Britain controlled the world's trade in cotton textiles functioned well as intermediaries between producers and markets, and indeed provided a fair slice of the empirical background to nineteenth-century economic thought, should have failed to function effectively in a changed market situation. But the way in which so many new developments in textile marketing—mail order houses and multiple stores, and the growth of branded products, are among the most important—are compelling changes in the weaver-finisher-merchant converter structure makes it clear that this is no longer appropriate.

A large number of small firms remain, however, and it would be hasty to conclude that none of them have a future, although it is currently fashionable to argue that what Lancashire needs is further amalgamation into at most two or three large groups. The assumption underlying this view would appear to be that only large groups can command the full range of technical and marketing skills, and the financial resources, needed to survive. But it is not necessarily the case that all the available managerial talent—the industry's scarcest resource—is best concentrated in large organizations. These, by their strength and financial standing, and the career opportunities they can offer, are always likely to attract a large share of it, but there are some people who prefer to work for themselves, and it is hard to see why there should be no room for such people in textiles, an industry with heterogeneous and ever-changing products. Indeed there obviously is room, and there have been remarkable individual successes.[1] The needs of small businesses have often been analysed: better technical services, improved access to finance, industrial training schemes (an Industrial Training Board for the textile industry has already been established). But what perhaps is needed most is a feel for the market, and the managerial and technical ability to adapt to its ever-changing demands.

[1] Sekers and Bernat Klein are two that come to mind. Is there any significance in the fact that the founders of both are foreign-born, and came into the British textile industry without any pre-conceptions as to how markets should be divided up?

APPENDIX

THE EFFECTS OF CONTRACTION IN TEXTILES ON THE ECONOMY OF THE NORTH-WEST

One important argument for special government assistance to the cotton industry, in the official view, was its geographical concentration. In the words of the White Paper, 'A special and compelling reason for seeking a solution to this problem is the geographical concentration of the industry in one area and its deep roots in, and great importance to, the life of the communities whose industrial history it has so largely made'. It is thus of interest to try to determine in what ways the Act has affected Lancashire's industrial structure and its employment position. These questions are also important in the broader context of national economic growth. Textile production is still a relatively labour-intensive industry, with net output per employee in 1963 only 61.5 per cent of the mean for all manufacturing industries, and the Act may have accelerated the transfer of labour to other more productive forms of employment.

There are formidable difficulties in the way of finding a firm or definitive answer to the questions posed. In the first place, the statistical material is fragmentary and unsystematic. The boundaries of D.E.A. regions and Ministry of Labour regions are not the same, and the Cotton Board's own statistics differ from both these in geographical coverage and in the way the industry is defined. It is thus impossible to relate Ministry of Labour and Cotton Board figures at all precisely. Furthermore, and more importantly, it is impossible to be sure just how far the changes that can be identified are due to the Act, and how far to other forces. Nevertheless there is a certain amount of evidence about the extent of the contraction in cotton and the accompanying changes in the area's industrial structure, that cumulatively permit some conclusions to be drawn.

I. THE DECLINE IN THE TEXTILE LABOUR FORCE

The peak post-war year for employment in 'Lancashire' textiles was 1951, when the industry employed over 360,000 people, according to the Cotton Board's statistics. Between the end of 1951 and the end of 1966 this labour force declined by 60 per cent, to 145,000. Figure A.1 shows the pattern of decline. After the 1952 recession there was some recovery in employment, but from 1954 onwards it has shrunk continuously, with some flattening out of the rate of decline in 1956-7, 1960-1, and 1963-4.

Figure A.1. Employment in Lancashire Textiles, 1951–66 (thousands)

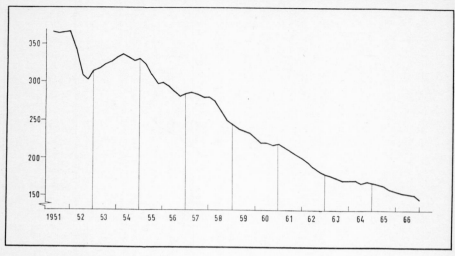

Source : Cotton Board.
Note : Data are for numbers on books in spinning, waste spinning, doubling in the United Kingdom, and in weaving for the Lancashire area only, plus numbers at work in weaving in the rest of the U.K. and in finishing in Great Britain only. (Numbers on books, end quarter ; numbers at work, quarterly averages.)

Figure A.2. Numbers on the books and numbers at work (excluding finishing), end year, 1951–66 (thousands)

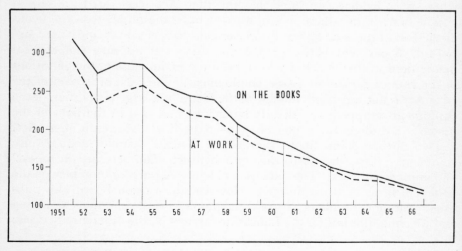

Source : Cotton Board.

H

Figure A.3.   Men as percentage of total employees, 1951–66, spinning and weaving only

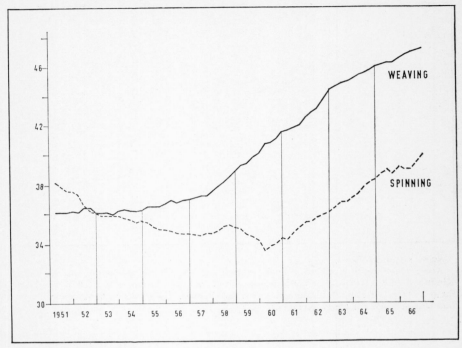

Source : Cotton Board.

There is no evidence to show that the 1959 Act accelerated the rate of contraction: in fact the opposite was the case, the number on the books at the end of the year falling by 13 per cent between 1957 and 1958, and by only 8 per cent between 1958 and 1959. It appears that cyclical fluctuations in textile activity have been the main cause of the variations in the rate of decline in textile employment. The lack of impact of the 1959 Act is not surprising in view of the fact that a large proportion of the equipment scrapped was already lying idle, and also in the light of the up-turn in trade in the winter of 1959–60, itself partly a result of the Act.

Two further points about the decline in textile employment require comment. First, the narrowing gap between 'numbers on the books' and numbers at work. The data used in figure A.1 are for 'numbers on the books' of firms in the industry.[1] However the Cotton Board also publishes series for 'numbers at work' in spinning, waste spinning, doubling and weaving, this last for the Lancashire area only, the difference between

---

[1] Except for finishing, where the only data available are for the numbers at work.

the two series representing people laid off for temporary stoppages of various kinds. Since 1960, as figure A.2 shows, the gap between numbers on the books and numbers at work has averaged 4 per cent per annum, compared with 10 per cent per annum in the preceding ten years. This change suggests that labour is now being more fully used, and taken with all the other evidence about the general labour situation in Lancashire is an indication of the way the 'labour shortage' has made itself felt in textiles.

A second interesting point is the change in the sex-composition of the labour force. The proportion of men employed in weaving has been rising since the mid-1950's, and in spinning since the end of 1959. These changes are shown graphically in figure A.3. Two reasons for them can be identified. First, for weaving, there is a technical factor, in that automatic looms, and in particular the most modern types of weaving machines such as the Sulzer, both require a much smaller labour force to operate them—and the actual job of weaving is traditionally a female occupation—and require a relatively larger maintenance force with engineering skills. A similar technical explanation may partly account for the change in spinning since 1960. In the 1950's there was a contrary factor at work in the shape of a rapid decline in the numbers of mule spindles, traditionally worked by men, and a consequent increase in the proportion of ring spindles, worked by women.

Another important factor for both spinning and weaving is the growth of shift working, in particular three-shift working, as the employment of women on a night shift is forbidden by law. Between 1961 (the earliest year for which figures are available) and 1966 the proportion of spindles running on more than one shift increased from 23.2 per cent to 49.3 per cent, and the proportion of looms from 31.3 per cent to 40.8 per cent. By 1966, 13.8 per cent of spindles and 19.9 per cent of looms were being operated on three shifts, the rapid growth of night working in spinning being especially striking.

Table A.1. *Extent of shift working, spinning and weaving, 1961–6[a]*

	1961	1962	1963	1964	1965	1966
Spindles						
Percentage running 2 shifts	20.9	21.4	25.5	32.2	33.8	35.5
Percentage running 3 shifts	2.3	3.3	6.2	8.8	11.5	13.8
Looms						
Percentage running 2 shifts	20.6	21.9	22.7	22.4	21.3	20.9
Percentage running 3 shifts	10.7	10.6	13.5	16.4	17.8	19.9

Source : Cotton Board.

[a] Data for spinning are for the United Kingdom; data for weaving for Great Britain only.

2. CHANGES IN THE LABOUR FORCE IN THE LANCASHIRE AREA

Between 1959 and 1964 the total number of employees in Lancashire grew by 1.4 per cent, according to Ministry of Labour figures. This small increase in total growth however conceals some large changes for individual industries and categories of employment, as table A2 shows. Among shrinking industries, agriculture and mining and quarrying contracted most rapidly, though accounting for only a small proportion of total employment anyway, closely followed by textiles, where the number of employees fell by 22 per cent. The service industries expanded fastest, accounting for over 23 per cent of total employment by 1964, and they were followed by construction, miscellaneous manufacturing industries—of which the paper, printing and publishing group grew most rapidly—and the metal using industries.

The table also shows that textiles, although no longer the main industry in Lancashire, still accounts for a significant proportion of total employment, at 8.3 per cent, or 18 per cent of manufacturing employment. Such data, however, considerably understate the importance of textiles to certain areas within the county. An approximate estimate, based on data provided for the North West regional study, suggests that in the main textile areas—Mid-Lancashire, North Manchester and North East Lancashire—textiles accounted for between 15 and 30 per cent of total employment.[1] And for individual towns, particularly in North East Lancashire, the degree of dependence on textiles is still greater than this.[2]

The total number employed in all industries in these three main textile areas is estimated to have fallen by about 4.5 per cent between 1953 and 1963, with the greatest fall, of over 10 per cent, occurring in North East Lancashire. But unemployment rates have not risen, partly because of outward migration from these areas and partly because of the decline in the number of people of working ages in their populations, as younger people leave.[3] Table A.3 shows total changes in population between 1951 and 1964 for the North West Region as a whole and for the main textile areas, sub-divided according to the North West Study Group area classification. In two of these sub-divisions, Blackburn and Burnley,

[1] Department of Economic Affairs, *The North West, a Regional Study* (H.M.S.O. 1965) p. 42.

[2] As recently as 1954, 8 districts in the North West had a third or more of their total insured labour force employed in Lancashire textiles (Cotton Board definition) : Darwen (33 per cent), Rochdale (35), Colne (42), Padiham (43), Nelson (50), Royton (69) and, in the West Riding, Todmorden (44), and in Derbyshire, Glossop (53). See Robson, *The Cotton Industry in Britain, op. cit.* p. 44.

[3] Department of Economic Affairs *op. cit.*, p. 45. Between 1951 and 1961 the proportion of the total population of working age (i.e. between 15 and retiring age) fell by 2 per cent in the North West, in contrast with an increase of rather less than 2 per cent in Great Britain.

Table A.2. *Lancashire: estimated numbers of employees in main industry groups, 1959–64, at June each year*

Nos. thousands

| | 1959 | | 1960 | | 1961 | | 1962 | | 1963 | | 1964 | | Percentage change over |
	Number	% Total	Number	% Total	Number	% Total	Number	% Total	Number	% Total	Number	% Total	whole period
Manufacturing													
Food, drink, tobacco	109	4.4	109	4.4	109	4.4	110	4.4	109	4.4	107	4.3	− 2
Chemicals	86	3.5	87	3.5	83	3.3	84	3.4	82	3.3	79	3.2	− 8
Metal using industry	416	16.9	433	17.5	446	17.9	449	18.0	443	17.8	451	18.1	+ 8
Textiles	267	10.9	255	10.3	244	9.8	225	9.0	211	8.5	207	8.3	−22
Other manufacturing	280	11.4	292	11.8	295	11.9	291	11.7	290	11.7	302	12.1	+ 8
All manufacturing	1,159	47.1	1,177	47.5	1,176	47.3	1,158	46.5	1,134	45.7	1,146	46.0	− 1
Agriculture, forestry, fishing, mining, quarrying	73	3.0	66	2.7	61	2.4	59	2.3	59	2.3	53	2.1	−27
Construction	132	5.4	134	5.4	140	5.6	144	5.8	148	6.0	145	5.8	+10
Distributive trades	322	13.1	327	13.2	330	13.2	332	13.3	333	13.4	334	13.4	+ 4
All other services	774	31.5	774	31.4	781	31.4	802	31.9	810	32.7	821	32.8	+ 6
All industries and services	2,459	100	2,478	100	2,488	100	2,495	100	2,481	100	2,493	100	+ 1

Source : Ministry of Labour.

H*

the total fall in population has been greater than the net loss from migration, the number of deaths exceeding the number of births, and there
was also an excess of deaths over births in the Rossendale area, although
this was offset by ex-servicemen returning to civilian employment.

Because the decline in employment in the textile areas has been
accompanied by a fall in population in most of them, unemployment has
not risen high enough to result in the establishment of any development
districts under the 1960 Local Employment Act,[1] which has added to the
difficulties of attracting new industries to towns and villages that are poor
in social capital and modern industrial and living facilities to start with.

Table A.3.   *North-West Region and selected sub-regions, population
changes 1951–64*

	Population (thousands)		Percentage change
	1951	1964	
North-West Region	6,380.0	6,661.9	
Sub-regions			
Oldham	245.8	237.5	− *8.3*
Bolton	236.3	234.6	− *1.7*
Bury	144.2	152.4	+ *8.3*
Rochdale	119.0	116.6	− *2.4*
Leigh	86.9	83.4	− *3.4*
Stalybridge	64.8	64.0	+ *1.0*
High Peak	38.0	37.6	− *0.5*
Blackburn	256.3	251.2	− *5.1*
Preston	203.7	220.8	+ *17.1*
Burnley	179.3	169.8	− *9.5*
Chorley	66.4	68.0	+ *1.6*
Rossendale	57.9	54.6	− *3.3*

Source : Department of Economic Affairs, *The North West, A Regional Study* (H.M.S.O.
1965), Appendix table 11.

3. THE CONVERSION OF COTTON MILLS

One important consequence of the contraction of the cotton industry
has been the creation of a pool of available industrial buildings.   It
has been pointed out that no part of the 'cotton' area of Lancashire has
qualified for special assistance from the central government since 1960[1]
and this has meant that the Board of Trade has not been liberal in
regarding it as eligible for specially lenient treatment in the granting of
Industrial Development Certificates for new building.   However, the
existence of textile mill buildings of all shapes and sizes, together with a
potential labour force, has made it possible for local authorities to attract
various new industries and activities that might otherwise not have
considered moving into the area.

The efforts of individual local authorities have been supplemented by

[1] From 1953 to 1960 North East Lancashire was scheduled as a Development Area under
the Distribution of Industry Act of 1945.

the work of the Lancashire and Merseyside Development Corporation, a body financed mainly by local authority contributions. L.A.M.I.D.A. began to promote the resale of cotton buildings in a systematic way in 1958, a year before the Act, and is continuing to do so with considerable success. The main attractions of the buildings are their low cost and the possibility they suggest of being able to recruit labour, particularly in the smaller towns and villages. On the other hand, many of the buildings are old and inconvenient—with narrow spaces between vertical pillars and inadequate lifts, for example, poor access and loading space, and poor communications. In addition some of them are on cramped sites offering little possibility for expansion, and the generally 'run-down' appearance of many Lancashire towns makes it difficult to persuade managers and their wives to move into them.

According to L.A.M.I.D.A's. estimates, which are based on a variety of sources, including local newspapers, and must be regarded as subject to a substantial margin of error,[1] over 850 mills have been closed between 1951 and 1964, 40 per cent of the closures being before 1959, 35 per cent under the reorganization schemes, and the remaining 25 per cent since 1960. There were a further 16 'chief' mill closures in 1965, and 47 mills, varying considerably in size, were closed in 1966.

Table A.4.   *Cotton mill closures in the North-West, 1951–64*

Sub-area	Main sectors of activity	Mills in operation 1951	Mills in operation 1964	Mills closed	% of 1951 total closed by 1964	Number re-occupied	% of closed mills re-occupied
Blackburn	W	140	58	82	59	69	84
Bolton	S	220	95	125	57	90	72
Accrington	W	70	31	39	56	30	77
N.E. Lancs	W	271	96	121	56	101	83
S. Lancs	S	77	35	42	55	26	62
Oldham	S	237	109	128	54	83	65
Chorley	W	39	19	20	51	17	85
Stockport	F/S	85	46	39	46	30	77
Manchester	F	141	81	60	43	51	85
Ashton-u-Lyme	S	83	49	34	41	31	91
Preston	W	72	44	28	39	21	75
Rossendale	W	91	56	35	38	25	71
Bury	W/F	177	114	63	36	45	71
Rochdale	S	136	100	46	31	35	76
Total, all Sub-areas		1,795	934	861	48	654	76

Source : Lancashire and Merseyside Development Corporation.
Notes : The sub-areas comprise the towns named and neighbouring villages and districts.
F — Finishing, S — Spinning, W — Weaving.

[1] In that they probably *understate* the number of closures, as not all closures get reported or otherwise notified to L.A.M.I.D.A.

Table A.4 shows how these closures were distributed among the main manufacturing districts, which have been ranked in order of the percentage of mills closed, with the areas with the largest proportion of closures at the top. No information on either numbers employed or physical size is available that would permit a weighting of the data, which cannot therefore be used to measure the change in the dependence of the different areas on textiles as a field of employment. The right-hand columns of the table give the numbers of mills re-occupied for other purposes than textile production, expressed as an absolute and as a percentage of mills closed. In the whole area covered by the figures,[1] about 76 per cent of the mills have been re-occupied. A further 15 per cent were vacant (in November 1964) and 9 per cent had been demolished. At the end of 1965 there were 147 vacant mills, compared with 127 in November 1964. The figures do not suggest that a higher proportion of the mills has closed in the weaving areas than in the spinning areas, or vice versa, nor do they point to any important variations in the proportion of mills re-occupied. Of the two areas furthest from the growth point of Manchester and the line of communications created by the M.6 road, Rossendale has one of the lowest percentages of closures and the lowest percentage of re-occupancies during the period covered by the table, while North East Lancashire has a high percentage of closures and a very high rate of re-occupancy, over 80 per cent. But diversification began in the Rossendale area even before the first world war, and so the scope for further closures was probably not so great as in many other districts.

The availability of mill premises has been an important factor in attracting industry to the cotton areas. In 1965 the total area of existing premises re-occupied in the North West was 8.3 million square feet, of which 4.6 million square feet was former cotton mills. This figure compares with 9.3 million square feet of new factory building authorized in the same year. But paradoxically the very success of L.A.M.I.D.A. and individual local authorities in selling old cotton mills to new users, and so helping to keep unemployment low, may have limited the general progress of the area, given the way in which regional development legislation has been operated. In a paper published in June 1966 L.A.M.I.D.A. argued the case for a more positive policy of industrial expansion in the textile areas of Lancashire.

'Many of the towns of Central and East Lancashire have a substantial stock of buildings, many constructed well over a century ago, which are quite unsuitable for modern use, including not only houses but factories, offices, warehouses, schools and shops. The dismal and

---

[1] It includes parts of Cheshire, Derbyshire and the West Riding as well as Lancashire.

outdated appearance of many of these old industrial towns has been a further cause of migration, especially of the younger and more vigorous element of the population. Moreover, combined with Board of Trade restrictions on industrial development in this area, it has deterred some of the more progressive firms in the growth industries and expanding professional and distributive trades from developing in this part of the country.

A very high proportion of the industrial development that has taken place in these towns during the post-war years is housed in old cotton mills. Other former mills remain vacant and are often badly sited or near derelict. At present over 8 million square feet of industrial accommodation, mainly mill property, is vacant in Central and East Lancashire but if the environment is to be improved and industry made more efficient, many of these vacant old mills together with many of those in use, must be replaced by purpose-built modern factories. Industrial development certificates should be freely issued for the erection of factories on the sites of demolished mills.

As in North East Lancashire and Rossendale, unemployment is low and superficially all is well. Yet these towns are areas of only medium prosperity. Although their economic position is undoubtedly stronger than 10 or 15 years ago, their problems are by no means solved. Some further contraction of employment in the textile industry seems certain and a more balanced industrial structure is still required. New factories are few and far between and much of the old industrial, as well as residential property needs to be replaced by modern buildings.'[1]

By way of an example of the stultifying effect of the policy of restricting new building, the same paper quotes the refusal of the Board of Trade to grant an Industrial Development Certificate to a company wanting to build a new factory in the Rossendale Valley,[2] which as table A.3 shows has experienced a relatively high rate of population decline in recent years.

This whole line of argument points to the need to improve the quality of employment. Making sure that every man and woman of employable age has a job is not enough: the quality of these jobs must be improved, in order to ensure that each member of the working population is making his maximum contribution to national output. Taking net output per employee as a measure of the quality of employment offered by an industry, this means that labour needs to be encouraged to move to

[1] Lancashire and Merseyside Industrial Development Association (L.A.M.I.D.A.), *An Industrial Policy for the North West,* June 1966.
[2] L.A.M.I.D.A. *op. cit.,* Appendix I.

industries with a higher net output per employee, as well as from the less efficient to the more efficient firms within each industry. Either labour must move, or new industries must be attracted to the textile areas of the North West. And as, on the whole, industries with a higher net output per worker tend to pay higher wages, an inward movement of new enterprises might help to counteract outward migration.

For the North West as a whole, net output per employee in 1958 (the latest year for which a regional breakdown of Census of Production figures is available) was 95 per cent of the average for Great Britain, while employment income per tax unit in 1959/60 was 96 per cent of the average for the United Kingdom. However, average earnings (and net output per employee) in the textile areas of the region were probably substantially below the average regional level, in view of the fact that average earnings in the textile industry were only about 80 per cent of the national average for all manufacturing industries, and net output per person employed in textiles (including working proprietors) was only 71 per cent of the national average for all manufacturing industries.

No systematic detailed information is available on the changing structure of industry and employment in the 'cotton' towns. But the experience of a single town, Bolton, for which detailed data has been made available, is interesting to analyse. It is not suggested that Bolton can be regarded as a 'typical' textile town, not least because of the exceptional efforts it has made to diversify its industrial base, but it provides material for a case study of industrial change at a micro-economic level.

4. CHANGE IN A TEXTILE TOWN: BOLTON

The main facts about the changes in the population and employment structure of Bolton are set out in tables A.5 and A.6. Two facts about the total figures stand out: first, that there has been a very small decline in population, of less than 0.5 per cent, and a slightly larger decline of about 0.5 per cent in the insured population, and second, that except in the year 1958 the unemployment percentage has been below the North West regional average, and, since 1960, at or below the national average. The fall in insured population has all been in women, the number of men insured increasing by over 1 per cent.

Table A.6 summarizes the changes between 1955 and 1965 in numbers employed in the leading industrial groups active in the town. Among the main manufacturing industries, the increase of 2,400 in the metal using group of industries was not large enough to compensate for the fall of 11,200 in textiles, and total employment in manufacturing industry fell by 16 per cent. This was largely offset by increases in employment of

Table A.5. *Bolton employment area:*[a] *population, insured population, and average percentage unemployed, 1955–64*

	1955	1956	1957	1958	1959	1960	1961	1962	1963	1964	Nos. thousands % change
Total population	175.9	174.8	174.0	173.1	173.1	172.9	174.8	175.4	175.5	175.6	−0.5
Insured population											
Men	47.8	47.6	47.6	47.5	46.3	47.8	48.6	48.7	48.4	48.3	+1.0
Women	35.1	34.9	35.8	33.9	33.4	34.8	34.7	33.9	32.7	34.2	−2.5
Total	82.9	82.6	83.4	81.3	79.7	82.6	83.3	82.6	81.1	82.5	−0.5
Average percentage unemployed	1.3	0.8	0.8	2.8	2.5	1.4	1.3	1.8	2.5	1.5	
N.W. region	1.4	1.3	1.6	2.7	2.8	2.0	1.6	2.5	3.1	2.1	
Great Britain	1.1	1.2	1.4	2.1	2.3	1.6	1.6	1.9	2.5	1.7	

Source : Official estimates made available by the Borough of Bolton.

[a] The Bolton employment area comprises the County Borough of Bolton and the Urban District of Turton.

Table A.6.   *Bolton employment area: employment by main industry groups, June 1955 and June 1965*

	June 1955 Number	% total	June 1965 Number	% total	Percentage change
Manufacturing					
Food, drink & tobacco	2,406	2.9	2,338	2.9	− 3
Chemicals	1,167	1.4	1,437	1.8	+23
Metal using industries	14,883	18.0	17,309	21.4	+16
Textiles	28,994	35.0	17,827	22.1	−38
Other manufacturing	6,978	8.4	6,790	8.4	− 3
All manufacturing	54,428	65.7	45,701	56.6	−16
Construction	4,192	5.1	4,621	5.7	+10
Distributive trades	6,241	7.5	9,995	12.4	+60
All other services	17,281	20.8	20,234	25.2	+17
All industries and services	82,876	100	80,755	100	− 3

Source : Ministry of Labour estimates.

3,800 in the distributive trades (a rise of 60 per cent), and 3,000 in services, including 1,700 in professional and scientific services.

According to a list prepared for the Borough Industrial and Development Sub-Committee, 71 mills were closed between 1957 and December 1965. L.A.M.I.D.A. data on closures in the Bolton district, which are not completely comparable in geographical coverage or time span, indicate that rather more than half (54 per cent) of the listed mills were shut down under the 1959 Act, about 20 per cent before 1959 (including a number for which the date of closure is not known), and about 25 per cent since. Of the 71 units, 44 have been re-occupied by new non-textile users, 12 demolished (including one that was re-occupied for a period by a non-textile user first), 5 re-occupied after closure by textile firms, 3 vacant and the future of the remaining 7 still under negotiation. The same estimate suggests that the re-occupied mills, excluding those still occupied by textile users, provided about 4,000 jobs. It is not possible to classify the various new occupants in great detail, but table A.7 shows the main types of users, with estimates of the number of people employed in each. The 'distribution' group included two mail order houses employing over 1,700 people. The 'multiple' users are very varied—one mill is listed as being occupied by almost 30 tenant firms for a variety of purposes including rainwear manufacture, shop-fittings, confectionery, photo-electric and electronic control equipment, cane baskets, engineering patterns, signs and light engineering products, also printing, wholesale and retail distribution, storage and offices.

Table A.7.   *Bolton: mill closures 1957 to December 1965, and subsequent use of mills*

	Number of units	Employment 1965 (estimated)
Mills re-occupied		
Manufacturing	24	2,800
Leased in sections	7	600
Textiles	5	300
Food Processing	3	300
Distribution	6	1,800
Storage	4	100
Demolished	12	—
Vacant	3	—
Under negotiation	7	—
Total	71	5,900

Source : Industrial Development Office, Borough of Bolton.

The re-occupied premises amounted to about half the 9 million square feet of factory space vacated since 1957: 1½ million square feet of space had been demolished, some of it by new owners planning to rebuild, some of it by the Borough for new housing and road schemes, and the rest was either vacant or under negotiation.

Apart from the decline in textiles, the main change in the pattern of employment in the town has been the growth of non-manufacturing employment, especially in distribution, although the proportion employed in construction and the service industries, 44 per cent in 1964, is still much lower than the average for Great Britain of 55 per cent. The fastest rate of expansion has been in distribution, as table A.6 shows. A Littlewoods mail order warehouse established in a former cotton mill in 1959 was estimated to provide 1,600 jobs in 1965, and in addition to this large single source of employment Bolton is a growing storage and distribution centre for a number of products.

Since 1955 the male insured population has grown by about 1 per cent while the female insured population has shrunk by about 3 per cent. Taken in conjunction with the low unemployment figures, this suggests that for men, at least, there has been no serious shortage of suitable new employment opportunities to offset the decline in textile employment. This has on the whole been the case, although according to the Borough's Industrial Development Officer there is a shortage of jobs for men with advanced technical skills, and a lack of apprenticeships and similar trade training facilities.

The fall in the number of women in the insured population is probably mainly due to the contraction of the textile industry. It is impossible to be sure how many of the women who lost their jobs as mills closed down are still unemployed, in the sense that they would take another job if a suitable one was offered. When married women lose their jobs many of them withdraw from the labour market altogether, rather than register at the labour exchange as unemployed, and thus a low unemployment percentage does not necessarily mean that there is no pool of unemployed labour, as some of the 'retired' women might take another job if one were offered them. The size of the potential reserve of female labour is probably never a fixed quantity: except in circumstances of great financial need the attitude of married women towards regular employment seems to be governed by the nature of the job, the pay and local custom.

STATISTICAL APPENDIX

The Cotton Board definition of the industry, as set out in the Cotton Industry Development Council order of 1948, relates to the processing of cotton fibre and man-made fibres of all types except those man-made fibres processed by woollen textile manufacturers. This in practice excludes man-made fibres with a staple length of 3 inches or more. The definition starts with the spinning process, and the inclusion of subsequent processes is determined by the proportion of cotton and man-made fibre spun yarn used in them. Thus *spinning* is defined as the production of single yarn containing not less than 95 per cent by weight of cotton, man-made fibre yarn of staple length not exceeding 3 inches, or any mixture of the two, and *weaving* as the production of woven cloth (other than narrow fabrics up to 18 inches in width) containing not less than 85 per cent of yarn produced in cotton spinning, continuous filament man-made fibre yarn, or any mixture of the two.[1]

Every person carrying on business in the industry, as defined, has to register with the Board, and can be legally compelled to make statistical returns to it. Thus in principle the statistical coverage for firms in the industry in Great Britain is complete. The Industrial Development Organization and Development Act of 1947, under which the Cotton Board was set up, does not apply to Northern Ireland and the Board has to depend on various sources of information in preparing its estimates of employment and production for the United Kingdom.

The main published series of statistics collected by the Board are for employment, machine activity, output and raw material consumption (cotton and staple fibre). The figures are all compiled on a sectional basis—there are separate series giving employment, machine activity and output for spinning, waste spinning, doubling and weaving, and series on employment and output for finishing.[2][3]

Information collected by the Cotton Board has the advantage of internal consistency: the different series relate to the same productive units over the same period of time. But they cannot reaily be used in conjunction with other sources of industrial statistics, such as the Census of Production and the Ministry of Labour's employment statistics, mainly

---

[1] When in January 1967 the Cotton Board was wound up and replaced by the Textile Council, the definition of the industry was extended to include several important new processes, notably warp knitting and yarn bulking. The period covered by the present study does not include this latest development.

[2] For details of the Cotton Board's statistical activities and a picture of the full extent of statistical information about the industry, see 'Statistics of the Cotton Industry' by D. C. Shaw, Director of Statistics at The Cotton Board, in *The Statistician*, vol. 14, no. 1 (1964).

[3] All published in the *Quarterly Statistical Bulletin*, which also gives extensive import and export statistics for the United Kingdom and other countries, drawn from a variety of sources.

because the latter adopt a significantly broader definition of the industry, including narrow fabrics, sewing thread, all textile finishing (not just the finishing of cotton and man-made fibre textiles) and the whole of the silk[1] and linen industries.

The main difficulty for the purposes of the present study, however, was that no measure of the structural pattern and the degree of integration could be derived from the available material. In order to obtain such a measure, it was necessary to work from the original data sent in by firms, from which the activities of each firm as indicated by its code number could be identified and the employment data classified by activity. The actual coding used by the Cotton Board, and the simplified classification used in the present study, are shown in table S.A.1. This was a laborious exercise, and could only be carried out for two points in time: April 1959, immediately before the introduction of the 1959 Act scrapping schemes, and 1964/65,[2] when re-equipment grant payments were being completed.

A detailed analysis of the types and sizes of firms participating in the scrapping schemes of the 1959 Act is provided in table S.A.2. This amplifies the text tables in chapter 4.

Table S.A.3 shows the structure of the industry in 1959 after the elimination of 'Premium Rate' firms, and in 1964/65, by type of activity and size range of firm.

---

[1] The new Textile Council embraces the silk industry, as well as the cotton and man-made fibre industries.

[2] For an explanation of the reason for this double date (employment in October 1964 classified by the structure of firms in October 1965), see chapter 4 p. 63.

Table S.A.1. *Relationship between Cotton Board classification of firms and classification used in this study*

Present classification		Cotton Board Classification Code Numbers	
		1959	1965
Single-process firms			
Spinners	Spinner	1	01
	Spinner, waste spinner	5	06
	Spinner, doubler	6	07
	Spinner, waste spinner, doubler	9	10
Waste spinners	Waste spinner	2	02
Doublers	Doubler	3	03
	Waste spinner, doubler	16	17
	Doubler, converter	—	24
Weavers	Weaver	4	04
	Waste spinner, weaver	17	18
	Waste spinner, weaver, converter	18	19
	Weaver, converter	24 ⎫	
	Weaver, converter	25 ⎬	25
	Weaver, converter	26 ⎭	
	Waste spinner, doubler, weaver	19	20
	Waste spinner, doubler, weaver, converter	20	21
	Doubler, weaver	21	22
	Doubler, weaver, converter	22	23
Finishers	Finisher	30	05
	Finisher, converter	—	29
Multi-process firms			
	Spinner, weaver	7	08
	Spinner, weaver, converter	8	09
	Spinner, waste spinner, weaver	10	11
	Spinner, waste spinner, weaver, converter	11	12
	Spinner, doubler, weaver	12	13
	Spinner, doubler, weaver, converter	13	14
	Spinner, waste spinner, doubler, weaver	14	15
	Spinner, waste spinner, doubler, weaver, converter	15	16

Table S.A.2. *Numbers of firms in the Lancashire textile industry at April 1959, and numbers participating in scrapping schemes, by size range and activity*

Size range (employment)	No. and size at 24.4.59		Firms scrapping equipment 'Premium Rate'		'Other'		Non-applicants	
	No.	Employment	No.	Employment	No.	Employment	No.	Employment
Single-process firms								
Spinners								
0	2	—	1	—	1	—	—	—
1–500	67	16,071	34	7,242	18	5,027	15	3,822
501–1000	13	9,022	1	953	11	7,386	1	683
1001–2000	2	2,389	—	—	2	2,389	—	—
2001 and over	2	5,924	—	—	1	3,007	1	2,917
Total	86	33,426	36	8,195	33	17,809	17	7,422
Doublers								
0	5	—	1	—	4	—	—	—
1–500	68	4,079	6	316	15	992	47	2,771
501–1000	2	1,434	—	—	1	779	1	655
Total	75	5,513	7	316	20	1,771	48	3,426
Weavers								
0	27	—	3	—	18	—	6	—
1–500	519	53,558	116	9,979	152	20,022	251	23,557
501–1000	17	11,713	4	2,410	11	7,598	2	1,705
1001–2000	4	6,171	—	—	2	2,508	2	3,663
Total	567	71,442	123	12,389	183	30,128	261	28,925
Finishers								
0	2	—	1	—	1	—	—	—
1–500	164	13,577	27	1,967	6	738	131	10,872
501–1000	7	4,618	2	1,553	1	522	4	2,543
1001–2000	2	2,098	—	—	2	2,098	—	—
2001 and over	2	7,358	—	—	2	7,358	—	—
Total	177	27,651	30	3,520	12	10,716	135	13,415
All single-process firms								
0	36	—	6	—	24	—	6	—
1–500	841[a]	88,874[a]	183	19,504	191	26,779	467[a]	42,591[a]
501–1000	39	26,787	7	4,916	24	16,285	8	5,586
1001–2000	8	10,658	—	—	6	6,995	2	3,663
2001 and over	4	13,282	—	—	3	10,365	1	2,917
Total	928	139,601	196	24,420	248	60,424	484	54,757
Multi-process firms								
0	1	—	—	—	1	—	—	—
1–500	14	4,104	4	1,082	10	3,022	—	—
501–1000	18	13,146	3	2,295	13	9,600	2	1,251
1001–2000	8	12,184	—	—	8	12,184	—	—
2001 and over	17	71,842	—	—	16	68,483	1	3,359
Total	58	101,276	7	3,377	48	93,289	3	4,610
All firms								
0	37	—	6	—	25	—	6	—
1–500	855[a]	92,978[a]	187	20,586	201	29,801	467[a]	42,951[a]
501–1000	57	39,933	10	7,211	37	25,885	10	6,837
1001–2000	16	22,842	—	—	14	19,179	2	3,663
2001 and over	21	85,124	—	—	19	78,848	2	6,276
Total	986	240,877	203	27,797	296	153,713	487	59,367

[a] Including 23 waste spinning firms, total employment 1569. There were no waste spinning firms with more than 500 employees.

Table S.A.3. *Changes in structure between 1959 (after elimination of 'premium rate, firms) and 1964/65, by size range and activity*

Size range (employment)	1959 (After elimination of 'premium rate' firms)		1964/65		Change 1959– 1964/65
	Number	Employment	Number (October 1965)	Employment (October 1964)	Number
Single-process firms					
Spinners					
0	1	—	2	—	+ 1
1–500	33	8,849	30	8,010	− 3
501–1000	12	8,069	8	5,332	− 4
1001–2000	2	2,389	1	1,104	− 1
2001 and over	2	5,924	—	—	− 2
Total	50	25,231	41	14,446	− 9
Doublers					
0	4	—	—	—	− 4
1–500	62	3,763	44	2,478	−18
501–1000	2	1,434	—	—	− 2
1001 and over	—	—	1	1,192	+ 1
Total	68	5,197	45	3,670	−23
Weavers					
0	24	—	6	—	−18
1–500	403	43,579	308	34,645	−95
501–1000	13	9,303	6	4,567	− 7
1001–2000	4	6,171	1	1,115	− 3
2001 and over	—	—	1	4,848	+ 1
Total	444	59,053	322	45,175	−122
Finishers					
0	1	—	—	—	− 1
1–500	137	11,610	124	8,959	−13
501–1000	5	3,065	3	1,770	− 2
1001–2000	2	2,098	—	—	− 2
2001 and over	2	7,358	1	2,313	− 1
Total	147	24,131	128	13,042	−19
All single-process firms					
0	30	—	8	—	−22
1–500	635	69,370	506	54,092	−129
501–1000	32	21,871	17	11,669	−15
1001–2000	8	10,658	3	3,411	− 5
2001 and over	4	13,282	2	7,161	− 2
Total	709	115,181	536	76,333	−173
Multi-process firms					
0	1	—	—	—	− 1
1–500	10	3,022	11	2,978	+ 1
501–1000	15	10,851	11	7,393	− 4
1001–2000	8	12,184	10	14,716	+ 2
2001 and over	17	71,842	7	62,918	−10
Total	51	97,899	39	88,003	−12
All firms					
0	31	—	8	—	−23
1–500	645	72,392	517	57,070	−128
501–1000	47	32,722	28	19,062	−19
1001–2000	16	22,842	13	18,127	− 3
2001 and over	21	85,124	9	70,079	−12
Total	760	213,080	575	164,338	−185

PUBLICATIONS OF THE
NATIONAL INSTITUTE OF ECONOMIC
AND SOCIAL RESEARCH

published by

THE CAMBRIDGE UNIVERSITY PRESS

Books published for the Institute by the Cambridge University Press are available through the ordinary booksellers. They appear in the three series below.

ECONOMIC & SOCIAL STUDIES

*I   *Studies in the National Income, 1924–1938*
     Edited by A. L. BOWLEY. Reprinted with corrections, 1944. pp. 256. 15s. net.

*II   *The Burden of British Taxation*
     By G. FINDLAY SHIRRAS and L. ROSTAS. 1942. pp. 140. 17s. 6d. net.

*III   *Trade Regulations and Commercial Policy of the United Kingdom*
     By the RESEARCH STAFF OF THE NATIONAL INSTITUTE OF ECONOMIC AND SOCIAL RESEARCH. 1943. pp. 275. 17s. 6d. net.

*IV   *National Health Insurance : A Critical Study*
     By HERMANN LEVY. 1944. pp. 356. 21s. net.

*V   *The Development of the Soviet Economic System : An Essay on the Experience of Planning in the U.S.S.R.*
     By ALEXANDER BAYKOV. 1946. pp. 530. 45s. net.

*VI   *Studies in Financial Organization*
     By T. BALOGH. 1948. pp. 328. 40s. net.

*VII   *Investment, Location, and Size of Plant: A Realistic Inquiry into the Structure of British and American Industries*
     By P. SARGANT FLORENCE, assisted by W. BALDAMUS. 1948. pp. 230. 21s. net.

VIII   *A Statistical Analysis of Advertising Expenditure and of the Revenue of the Press*
     By NICHOLAS KALDOR and RODNEY SILVERMAN. 1948. pp. 200. 25s. net.

*IX   *The Distribution of Consumer Goods*
     By JAMES B. JEFFERYS, assisted by MARGARET MACCOLL and G. L. LEVETT. 1950. pp. 430. 50s. net.

*X   *Lessons of the British War Economy*
     Edited by D. N. CHESTER. 1951. pp. 260. 30s. net.

*XI   *Colonial Social Accounting*
     By PHYLLIS DEANE. 1953. pp. 360. 60s. net.

*XII   *Migration and Economic Growth*
     By BRINLEY THOMAS. 1954. pp. 384. 50s. net.

*XIII   *Retail Trading in Britain, 1850–1950*
     By JAMES B. JEFFERYS. 1954. pp. 490. 60s. net.

XIV   *British Economic Statistics*
     By CHARLES CARTER and A. D. ROY. 1954. pp. 192. 30s. net.

XV   *The Structure of British Industry: A Symposium*
     Edited by DUNCAN BURN. 1958. Vol. I. pp. 403. 55s. net. Vol. II. pp. 499. 63s. net.

*XVI   *Concentration in British Industry*
     By RICHARD EVELY and I. M. D. LITTLE. 1960. pp. 357. 63s. net.

*XVII   *Studies in Company Finance*
     Edited by BRIAN TEW and R. F. HENDERSON. 1959. pp. 301. 40s. net.

XVIII   *British Industrialists: Steel and Hosiery, 1850–1950*
     By CHARLOTTE ERICKSON. 1959. pp. 276. 45s. net.

XIX   *The Antitrust Laws of the U.S.A.: A Study of Competition Enforced by Law*
     By A. D. NEALE. 1960. pp. 516. 50s. net.

* At present out of print.

* At present out of print.

STUDIES IN THE NATIONAL INCOME AND EXPENDITURE OF THE UNITED KINGDOM

Published under the joint auspices of the National Institute and the Department of Applied Economics, Cambridge.

1 *The Measurement of Consumers' Expenditure and Behaviour in the United Kingdom, 1920–1938*, vol. I
   By RICHARD STONE, assisted by D. A. ROWE and by W, J. CORLETT, RENEE HURSTFIELD, MURIEL POTTER. 1954. pp. 448. £7 10s. net.

2 *The Measurement of Consumers' Expenditure and Behaviour in the United Kingdom, 1920–1938*, vol. II
   By RICHARD STONE and D. A. ROWE. 1966. pp. 164. 90s. net.

3 *Consumers' Expenditure in the United Kingdom, 1900–1919*
   By A. R. PREST, assisted by A. A. ADAMS. 1954. pp. 196. 55s. net.

4 *Domestic Capital Formation in the United Kingdom, 1920–1938*
   By C. H. FEINSTEIN. 1965. pp. 284. 90s. net.

5 *Wages and Salaries in the United Kingdom, 1920–1938*
   By AGATHA CHAPMAN, assisted by ROSE KNIGHT. 1953. pp. 254. 75s. net.

THE NATIONAL INSTITUTE OF ECONOMIC AND SOCIAL RESEARCH

publishes regularly

THE NATIONAL INSTITUTE ECONOMIC REVIEW

A quarterly Review of the economic situation and prospects.
Annual subscription £2 10s.; single issues 15s. each.

The Review is available directly from N.I.E.S.R.
2, Dean Trench St., Smith Square, London, S.W.1

The Institute has also published

FACTORY LOCATION AND INDUSTRIAL MOVEMENT: a Study of Recent Experience in Britain, volumes I and II
By W. F. Luttrell
N.I.E.S.R. 1962. pp. 1080. £5 5s. net the set.

TRANSLATED MONOGRAPHS: A NEW SERIES ON CURRENT ECONOMIC PROBLEMS AND POLICIES

No. I *The IVth French Plan* by FRANCOIS PERROUX, with the original foreword by Pierre Massé, Commissaire Général au Plan, and a new foreword to the English edition by Vera Lutz. Translated by Bruno Leblanc.
N.I.E.S.R. 1965. pp. 72. 10s. net.

These are also available directly from the Institute.